# David's Story

## Tales of Life and Love Returning

David E. Cox

Grosvenor House
Publishing Limited

This book is published by
Grosvenor House Publishing Ltd
Link House
140 The Broadway, Tolworth, Surrey, KT6 7HT.
www.grosvenorhousepublishing.co.uk

A CIP record for this book
is available from the British Library

ISBN 978-1-83615-241-5

*For Parinya*

# CONTENTS

# INTRODUCTION

There are many different tales to be told within *David's Story*, but the most important tale is about young love, loss and, later, about love returning. The tales, I hope, have also something to say about innocence and experience, dreams and realities, our culture and the wider world.

The early tales are about my beginnings, the family and then travelling the length and breadth of England. We had lived in a dozen places by the time I was 18 years of age and I had attended six different schools. I think that probably the travelling as much as the family shaped what I was to become.

The next tale is about education, especially once I began its most important stage at the London School of Economics (LSE). It was at LSE in the late 1960s that I developed some of my values and my beliefs and learnt something about society and politics.

The fourth tale is concerned with young friendships. There were four of us together in the final year of school and at college. These friendships were to end for various reasons soon afterwards.

The fifth tale is about political beliefs and the possibility of radical change. Starting with the worldwide student revolt in 1968 and opposition to the Vietnam War, this phase was to continue in some respects throughout the 1970s.

The sixth tale is about social work, mainly childcare in the East End of London. Such a lot was experienced and there is so much to remember.

The seventh tale is about young love, 'a brief, dreamy, kind delight', as W. B. Yeats has described it. It was overwhelming and life-changing, but in many ways it was inevitably not to last.

The eighth tale is about football and watching Nottingham Forest in Europe and at home. It is the tale of supporting and following a small city club that won the First Division Championship and the European Cup twice while managed by Brian Clough.

The ninth tale is about being back in Nottingham, working in childcare and then with people with learning disabilities, and a friendship of two people with very different personalities that was to start in Nottingham and has continued for the rest of our lives.

The tenth tale is about getting fit, running marathons and half marathons.

The eleventh tale is about being a manager and learning something about the art of management and the necessary skills.

The twelfth tale is about travelling again, this time worldwide and in so doing discovering new places to enjoy and appreciate.

The thirteenth tale is about a new job, love returning in more ways than one and learning the most important lessons about love.

The fourteenth tale is about my marriage and discovering a new world.

The fifteenth tale is about retirement, experiencing cancer, vulnerability, being faced with possible death and yet recovering.

The sixteenth tale is about my parents again, bereavement, and trying to give meaning to it all.

The seventeenth tale is about Saga or getting older. It examines the early twenty-first-century years.

The eighteenth tale is about my last planned move and a new home out of London with many new experiences.

The nineteenth tale is about the Covid-19 pandemic.

The twentieth tale is about the recent years together with my partner.

Finally, in the last section, I offer a few reflections on my story and what has been important to me. As well as reflecting on love and friendship, I list some of my heroes and/or anti-heroes, and those people I continue to admire.

# 1.
# BEGINNINGS

My parents, who both came from Bolton, had met before the Second World War, but just like for so many young couples, everything changed when Hitler invaded Poland.

My father, Alfred, was a bright boy who, despite obtaining a scholarship to Manchester Grammar School, had to commence work instead in the 1930s to support his own father (who was unemployed), his mother and the rest of the family. There were altogether nine brothers and sisters, two of whom died in childhood. The family was very much working class, although my father was always proud to claim that one of his ancestors was George Stephenson of the *Rocket* steam engine fame. I have never discovered to this day whether it was true or not. I was in fact not close to most of my father's family, although when my grandmother later married again, I recall liking her new husband Wilson. He once took me fishing on the River Trent when they came to visit. We had an enjoyable and relaxing day and caught a few fish. Our outing together made a significant impression on me. We also spent some time later with his sister Edith, especially on one occasion when we visited Cardiff where they lived to watch some of the Commonwealth Games in 1958. I would have been nine years old.

My father, before the Second World War, was a lay preacher and a supporter of Neville Chamberlain's policy of appeasement regarding Nazi Germany. However, when the war started he was soon conscripted into the army, and after basic training was shipped to Singapore. Subsequently, with the surrender of the Singapore base and the allied armies to the Japanese after only eight days of battle in February 1942, he was then to spend the rest of the war as a prisoner working on the Death Railway in Thailand. In many ways, it was a miracle he survived, and he was to return to the UK after the war, emaciated and little more than a skeleton. He never really talked later to my sister and I about this experience, but my mother learnt a little about what happened. Suffice it to say that he was seriously ill at times with malaria to the extent that on one occasion the Japanese guards got him to dig his own grave. Fortunately, it was not required. He did return to England, however, with an abiding loathing of the Japanese and with a considerable antipathy to Australians, who had been his fellow prisoners. When he returned, he had also lost his religious faith and was never to be involved with a church again. Nor did he ever wish to return to Thailand.

After the war, he worked in local government in the local county treasurer's department in Lancashire but studied at night school for his accountancy qualification. He passed all the exams and became a certified accountant. He was eventually to leave local government and work in the private sector for National Cash Register and other organisations involved in the beginnings of the computer industry.

Later in his life, as someone who believed in self-reliance and entrepreneurship, he also attempted twice to set up his own business. On each occasion, it failed after short periods, although I do not really understand what caused these failures. He seemed to get on well with many people but was rather an introverted man who did not easily express his feelings. I remember my mother saying it would have been better if he had stayed in the county treasurer's department where he would have had much more secure employment! It was because of the many changes in his employment that we were to move so frequently in my childhood.

Regarding my parents' aspirations, I was later to understand that my father was strongly motivated to better himself in terms of both an improved standard of living and a more middle-class status. At the same time, he would joke about my mother that 'she was born with a silver spoon in her mouth'. It was not true, but it had been the case that my father's family had been poorer.

My mother, Edna, was a state enrolled nurse at Winwick Infirmary when she met my father. Her family lived in a council house in Mackenzie Street, in Astley Bridge, Bolton. She was the second daughter in a family of five children. She would continue her nursing career on and off for many years after she got married, both in the public and later in the private sector. Her grandfather had at one time operated a small livery delivery business, but her father was now a driver for the local Co-operative Society. I liked my grandfather very much and I remember his warmth and sitting on his knees when I was young. I recall thinking much later that I had felt much closer to my grandfather than to my own father, even though I had only met him occasionally. I also liked my maternal grandmother, who was called Annie. She came across to me as kind and gentle. I was only much later to learn that her family had a skeleton in the cupboard. The oldest sibling Elsie had not been fathered by my grandfather. Annie had been pregnant by another man when my grandparents married. It had been kept a secret for many years. Unsurprisingly, Annie had taught her daughters when they were young, including my mother, to never trust a man!

My mother was very pretty with blonde hair. I can remember her telling me with some pleasure that a neighbour had once said of her that 'if ever a film star walked down Mackenzie Street, it was you, Edna'. During the war, she cared for many injured soldiers, some of whom inevitably fell in love with her. However, she waited for my father to come home. She was compassionate and caring but had a nervous disposition.

My own first memory when we moved from a village called Belmont near Bolton, Lancashire (where my parents lived when I was born) to Wigan, not far away, was of a weekly bath in front of the coal fire in a tin tub. I could have been no more than three years old. Our home at that time in Wigan was a council house.

Other early memories include missing my mother very much when she was in hospital giving birth to my sister Elaine, but also at first not being sure it was her when she returned home. I think I was also angry with her that she had left me. My mother also told me that I feared the noise of the vacuum cleaner!

When I was four years old, we moved to another council house in St Helens near Liverpool. We were on top of a hill with a lot of wasteland in front of us where we could play. A lot of children played games there and I remember looking at this land with the children playing and imagining they were pirates coming to invade us. I also recall being with my father during warm weather when he built a new rock garden at the front of the house. I was fascinated by the way he built it, and all the interesting plants. Unfortunately, his commitment to gardening did not transfer to me and in my later life; I have had to rely on my partner to plan and look after our own garden!

My first primary school was in St Helens. In one lesson I recall receiving a gold star and having to go to see the headteacher to tell her. I was immensely proud.

It seemed such a big school, but many years later I remember visiting it out of curiosity and realising just how small it was.

When I was only five years old, we moved to Whitley Bay on the coast, just north of Newcastle upon Tyne. It was very pleasant being by the seaside, but the winter was so much colder than in Lancashire and there was such a lot of snow. I was a bit scared, as the snow seemed to come up to the top of my legs. My second school was there in Whitley Bay and I hated it, as they made you eat all the school dinner, whatever it was. I remember having to stuff potatoes and vegetables into my trouser pocket and feeling sick when I was told that I must finish everything. The experience gave me an aversion to some vegetables, especially carrots and beetroot. The aversion has lasted all my life. It was a terrible way to treat children.

I also went to my first football match when I was in Newcastle. My father took me to St James' Park and I stood on a box. I only recall the cheering when Newcastle came out on the pitch and the booing when the other side appeared. It was exciting, but I was a little scared at the same time. The early 1950s was a period when Newcastle United had an exciting and successful team. The same team is even now still waiting for the glory days to return, although they did have some success not too long ago with Kevin Keegan as manager, and they are currently playing well under Eddie Howe.

# 2.
# TRAVELLER

The family moved to Nottingham when I was still only five years old and my sister was two. By this stage, my father had bought an old Ford Anglia car and as we drove to Nottingham, my sister and I sang the words to 'Robin Hood':

'Feared by the bad, loved by the good, Robin Hood, Robin Hood, Robin Hood...'

We initially moved into a private flat in an old building in a village called Burton Joyce, north of Nottingham, in a road called, strangely, Willow Wong.

During the period that we lived there at Willow Wong, I remember we had a problem with mice. Various traps were set and poison was laid down. I recall that one night when I was in bed, I woke up to a rustling next to it. I had left some chocolate on the bedside table and one of the mice had been helping himself to the treat. On another occasion, we had been talking to the two older children of the doctor who lived next door about Father Christmas. They had asked Elaine and I whether we believed in him, and we had said we did. They responded by telling us that there was a Father Christmas down every chimney. Understandably, we were very puzzled. After thinking about it, I began to understand. However, I suppose it was not nice of them to attempt to undermine our belief at such young ages. At least my sister, Elaine, was too young at the time to appreciate the real meaning of what they had said.

Although we lived in three separate places during the six years we were in Burton Joyce, I remember this period as being the happiest of my childhood. First, we moved to a semi-detached house located centrally and then my parents later bought a detached house on a new development at the end of the village. The places and area where we lived were very pleasant and we were only a short walk away from the River Trent. My father worked long hours with a company, as I mentioned above, called National Cash Register (NCR) so in some respects he was a distant figure. I felt closer to my mother. I remember that she had a long fur coat and looked very pretty in it. I used to smuggle up to her coat when she was wearing it, which made me feel good. I also recall the smell of her perfume. I was only later to discover that it was Chanel No. 5. My parents also soon had good friends in the village who had children as well, so it seemed at times that we had an extended family.

Sometimes we would go for a walk in Bluebell Wood together. As a small child when the bluebells were out in April and May, it seemed to be a special magical place. I still think of bluebell woods in the same way today. On other occasions, we would call in at a farm owned by a family my mother knew. I remember one time sitting in the front room of their house in front of a roaring fire with one piglet next to it, which they were trying to revive. The piglet was almost being roasted in the attempt to keep it alive. My mother said it was the runt of the litter.

On Sundays, we always went out for a drive, often in the summer, to Sherwood Forest or Matlock Bath. When we went to Sherwood Forest the four of us would play cricket together, although my mother often opted out. We visited the Major Oak in Ollerton as well. This huge ancient oak tree was hollowed out and you could hide inside it. The myth was that Robin Hood had hidden there. We usually had an enjoyable time in Sherwood Forest, although on one occasion I remember jumping by accident into a bunch of stinging nettles. It was not a very pleasant experience. On another occasion, we found a giant mushroom, picked it, and brought it home with us. We planted it again and were rather disappointed when it failed to grow and shrivelled up. We did not understand that we had destroyed its thread-like hyphae. On other trips to Matlock Bath, we would climb the local hills, including the Heights of Abraham, and maybe have a meal out. This Sunday drive was like a ritual. My father also sometimes took me to watch Nottingham Forest play football at the City Ground. I will always remember the Robin Hood theme tune being played as the team ran on to pitch before the game. From that time, for all my life, I have always supported Nottingham Forest (see Chapter 8). We would occasionally go to watch the cricket at Trent Bridge as well. I recall going to the Test Match when England were playing the West Indies and being able to see the three W's: Worrell, Weekes, and Walcott batting. It was a lovely summer's day.

Elaine and I also played various games together, especially cowboys and Indians. I was the cowboy, and, as my younger sister, she was the Indian. I remember Elaine being dressed in an Indian outfit. Unsurprisingly, it was usually the case that the cowboy won! I was given plenty of toys to play with during my childhood. I remember having a toy fort and lots of soldiers with uniforms in many colours. I spent considerable time arranging them and determining which ones would succeed in the battle. Later, I had Scalextric racing cars with a track. I would sometimes compete with my father. The racing cars provided much entertainment. I was to have a bicycle a few years afterwards.

My parents arranged for me to join the Cubs at this time as well and I was soon collecting proficiency badges. I recall that I got one for learning to use the phone in the red phone box. At that time, you had a system of A and B phone buttons, so it was more complicated than it is at present. I remember that we used to go down regularly to play games next to the banks of the River Trent. I recall running there once and tripping over, with my face falling into a large cowpat. I needed quite a lot of cleaning up! If you did well at Cubs, you could become a Seconder or, better still, a Sixer. You were appointed to these positions because you were considered as being able to lead a team. I did manage to become a Seconder but did not progress any further. When I was 11 years old, I could have joined the Scouts but decided against it partly, I think, because I did not want to be with the bigger boys. I was perhaps unaware of the various opportunities the Scout movement could offer. Of course, neither at that stage did I have any understanding at all of Baden Powell's ideology as founder of the Scouts. Only when I was an adult did I become familiar with his racist and imperialist views.

All our parents' friends' children also went to the same primary school in the middle of the village. It was an old building with the usual design for the late Victorian or Edwardian periods. The toilets were at the other side of the playground. At this time, I recall getting on quite well at school and enjoying most of it. I did well with the schoolwork and remember as well playing British Bulldog in the playground, which could get quite physical at times as you tried to get from one end of the playground to the other without being tagged. I was also in the football team in my later years there, although on one occasion I was dropped, having been sent off previously for persistent fouling in a match against what I remember as bigger boys in nearby

Carlton. This was a disappointment to my father, who was a volunteer assistant coach for the team! It may have been partly due to this incident that my headmaster's report on leaving the school after I passed the eleven plus said that I was bright but needed to develop 'more of a sense of humour'! I was a serious child.

In the last year at my primary school, I had my first foreign trip to Belgium. The school arranged a short holiday to Knokke on the Belgian coast. I remember being on the beach and looking out to sea across the English Channel in the direction of England. We also visited Ostend and spent time viewing the casino. I can recall as well eating waffles, which I thought to be delicious. I was not homesick, but it was good to get back home after the trip.

Reflecting on my childhood in later life, it is clear to me that there was little emotional expression in our family, except for the nervousness of my mother. My father's emotions were rarely apparent and although he communicated to us about everyday matters, it was not possible to feel close to him, or indeed to feel his love for us. I do not doubt that he loved us, but there was rarely any emotional communication. However, I do remember one time when he came home drunk after work and there was an argument between my father and my mother while I was in bed, as was my sister. It was one of the few occasions in my childhood when my father was not really in control. My mother was really upset. By comparison, she was more able to express feelings and I felt closer to her. But such communication was hindered by her nervousness and her subservience to my father, who very much made all the major decisions. Nevertheless, it was always clear to me how much she loved and doted on me. Throughout our childhood, she always seemed closer to me than to my sister. I do remember enjoying different activities with my mother, such as walks, visiting friends and preparing food in the kitchen, with which Elaine was also involved. We always enjoyed licking the left-over dough in the bowl when cakes were made. My mother excelled in making cakes and she also regularly made a few special dishes, including Lancashire hotpot.

I would add that looking back I think there was limited humour in our house. We were quite a serious family. To the extent that there was humour, it was often led by my father, who would tease my mother about all sorts of things, but especially her allegedly more prosperous childhood.

Although I passed the eleven plus, I was told that in the three tests I had done, my marks were lower in my later tests, I think somewhat to the surprise of my teachers. Afterwards, when I went (as it turned out briefly) to Carlton-le-Willows Grammar School, I was not therefore in the highest stream. However, in most academic disciplines I was still top of my class but certainly far from being top across all the streams for the students in that year. In addition, in the non-academic subjects, such as art and woodwork, I was nearly always bottom of the class! I remember in a school report the woodwork teacher stating that 'he tries hard' and then giving me an E grade. I was also not so good at languages, including the English language lessons. This would result in some problems for me in later years after I got to university. The school played rugby and, owing to my small stature, I was chosen unsurprisingly for the scrum half position. I was to play several matches for the school.

After only two terms at my grammar school, the family moved again to a small village called Cropston, near Loughborough, in Leicestershire. It was a very pleasant village surrounded by rolling countryside. I soon had some friends and as I had acquired a bike, we would often cycle to nearby villages. My closest friend was called Peter.

I remember at about 13 years old being attracted to a girl called Linda and buying her some chocolates, but unfortunately for me, she was not interested in becoming my first girlfriend. I was very disappointed.

The family had a lovely collie dog during this period, which looked like Lassie and was called Kim, although his tail had been damaged, possibly in an accident. We had acquired him from a pet shop after a Labrador puppy my father bought for the family had died (after just three days). The collie had been bought as a replacement to help us recover from the upset. Elaine and I had the task of taking him for walks. Unfortunately, we were not as diligent as we should have been and were sometimes told off by our mother for not exercising him enough. Sometimes we took him on holiday with us. I remember us being with him in Sheringham, Norfolk, and having a lot of fun on top of some old air raid shelters until Kim jumped off a high one and nearly did himself serious damage. Fortunately, he was not injured and was soon up and running again. Much later, my mother was to sell the dog without telling us, as she still thought that no one had been taking him for sufficient walks. She was also to sell my sister's rabbit, again without informing us, on the grounds that she was not cleaning the cage enough.

During my childhood, we would usually have annual holidays by the seaside. In fact, we went to many seaside resorts across England and Wales, usually staying in Bed and Breakfast places. I can recall staying in some very odd places, including one house on the South Coast that seemed still to be furnished as it might have been in the Victorian era with a pot in which to relieve yourself under each bed. My father was keen to explore places. Additionally, on two occasions we stayed at holiday camps in Devon and at Prestatyn in North Wales. As a family, we enjoyed all these trips, although I can also remember that it always appeared to rain on our trips to Wales. It was when we were at a holiday camp there and still very young that we attended a fancy-dress evening and I was cast in the role of King Farouk, the corrupt and dissolute ex-King of Egypt. My father also played in a game of cricket. I remember him going out to bat and then being out first ball. It was a bit embarrassing for him.

Occasionally, we would visit members of my mother's family in Lancashire, especially her youngest sister, who was called Anne, and her husband, Don. They had a young son. I liked Anne and Don, who were both warm to me, and I recall that people in their village in Lancashire seemed more friendly than people where we lived. I also remember going out with them and flying a kite on the moors. The experience made a significant impression on me.

I attended a new school called Loughborough College School and continued to do quite well studying there. After a while, I also developed a new circle of friends. I recall early on in my second year, when I was sitting in the far corner desk in a maths lesson, having chalk thrown at me by the teacher because apparently I had not been concentrating. It was a bit of a shock. After all, I was only in the far corner because I had come top in the previous maths exam, and we were all positioned in the classroom according to how well we had done. Those who had come bottom or near bottom were in the front row. I also remember being punished during a gym lesson when the teacher hit me on my bottom with the end of one of the ropes. I do not recall what I was supposed to have done to deserve such treatment. This incident was the only time I was to be physically punished in my school career. Although punishment was often administered in the schools I attended, I was never to receive the cane.

Unlike Carlton-le-Willows, where I had played rugby for a while as scrum half, there was more football at Loughborough College School. I played the game sometimes but had no special talent for it. I only grew to five foot five inches, which did not help especially when tackling. However, it was in the academic subjects rather than at sport that I did well, winning several annual prizes, although I was still not in the top stream. My favourite subject was history. I remember doing a history exam in my third year when the instruction was to answer five out of the nine questions. Unfortunately, I misread this text and answered with some difficulty all nine questions in the time allotted. Therefore, they only counted my marks for the first five questions answered. But I still managed to get the top marks overall in the exam! However, I think it taught me an important lesson about reading exam instructions carefully!

The school had a boarding wing that specialised in admitting children whose parent(s) were in the armed forces. The headmaster was a huge man with a booming voice, but his wife was only tiny. They struck me as an odd pair.

I also remember in my third year running a cross-country race for third and fourth-year students and, as I did not know the course, falling from an overhanging cliff into a stream. I was soaked. There was a crowd watching and I was very embarrassed. Despite this mishap, to my surprise, (as I had done no training), I finished ninth overall, which was the best result for third year students. I had something of a pigeon chest, which my PE teacher for some reason felt was a good asset for long-distance running. However, it would be a long time in the future that I would start running again and finish undertaking some marathons.

It was also around that time that international politics and the Cold War interfered with my schooling. It was 1962 and the Cuban missile crisis. I did not really know what was going on, except that the adults considered it to be serious and that it was something to do with nuclear weapons. In the early afternoon, we were sent home to our parents in case nuclear war broke out. The crisis passed, as Khrushchev, the Soviet leader, backed down after Kennedy's ultimatum to remove the Soviet missiles in Cuba. We went back to school the next day.

At that time, and for another several years, I was attracted to another girl called Linda, who did take an interest in me. But I was far too shy to talk to her. I remember sitting in the library at school with Linda and her friend sitting opposite me, but we did not say a word to each other. However, some of my early sexual fantasies were about her. I remember once in the playground her skirt blowing up in the wind, exposing her petticoats and her stockings. This experience was certainly fuel for adolescent desire. However, my understanding of sexual feelings was very limited, as sex education at the school was non-existent until I was sixteen. It was not really any better at home, as my education consisted of being given a pamphlet on the 'birds and the bees'. It was embarrassing to wake up in bed some mornings with a hard-on and a discharge staining the sheets. I did not know that it was semen. Indeed, I did not know about masturbation either.

As a family, we continued most weekends to have an outing to local beauty spots, usually on a Sunday, as shopping in nearby Leicester tended to be the priority on a Saturday. Bradgate Park, which was nearby, was our favourite place to go. My father continued to be interested in sport, so he would take me to watch Leicester City on occasion, although I continued to support Nottingham Forest from afar and always watched out for their results (see Chapter 8). We also had the occasional longer-distance trips, including going to the Formula One Motor Racing Grand Prix one year when it was held at Aintree, Liverpool. I remember that the red Ferraris were triumphant that year. Additionally, as a pastime, I also started stamp collecting in my early teens and within a couple of years I had a good collection, although there was nothing that might be considered valuable!

Our family went on our first foreign package holiday when I was 14 years old. We travelled by coach across Europe to Diana Marina on the Italian Rivera near Genoa. On the way there, in Luxembourg, there was a serious incident in our hotel room when my sister asked me to scratch her back, as it was itching. In doing so, I scratched too hard, broke her skin, and left red wheals on her back. My father lost his temper completely and started beating me in a way he had never done before. Only when my mother begged him to stop did he finally do so. I had never seen my father behave in this way before and I was tearful and very shocked and upset. I deserved to be punished, but he had lost control. Looking back, his expression of anger I experienced on this occasion was probably his greatest expression of feeling towards me that I ever felt in the whole of my childhood. I have since wondered whether his anger on this occasion was at least in part triggered by his experience as a Japanese prisoner of war, when he would have seen people being punished. Of course, I apologised to my sister.

I continued to do well at most academic disciplines. Besides history, geography was another of my favourite subjects, partly as the teacher was very capable. We called him 'Slosher Brown' and he always made the subject interesting. He had already written textbooks for young people studying O Level GCEs and was later to become a school inspector. To punish pupils, he would sometimes make them stand on a little island in the middle of a small pond outside the class window, or even better, put them in a storage cupboard adjacent to the classroom. Sometimes more than one pupil would be put in the cupboard. I remember that some of us boys quite liked the idea of being put in the cupboard if a pretty girl was already there. On one occasion when I was walking the dog, I came across him hand in hand with our female biology teacher. I do not know who was most embarrassed! They were later to marry.

Sometime before I took my O Level GCEs at Loughborough College School, an incident occurred involving me, other students, and our form master, who it must be said was far from popular. It was a lunchtime, it was raining, and all the students wanted to get back in the classroom to shelter, but we were not allowed to.

As a kind of protest, a few of us then stood in front of the classroom door so that when our form master arrived, he found that his way was blocked. He then, instead of asking us to move, started hitting out at us and slapped me across the face. When I later approached him in the classroom and told him he could not behave like that, he tried to slap me again. I was going to talk to my parents about it, but soon after I got home, there was a reporter from the local newspaper at our door, as the parents of one of the other pupils had reported what had happened to the press. My mother allowed the reporter to interview me and it became the main story on the front page of the newspaper. The article was not factually accurate, but it obviously became a serious matter for the school. My parents were summoned to see the headteacher, but my father sided with the version that the school presented, which suggested the form teacher had been provoked. It was my behaviour and that of other students that was under scrutiny and deemed unacceptable. Nevertheless, our form teacher was moved from his position, which was a kind of success for the students. The incident also taught me to be suspicious in the future of the press, especially regarding the accuracy or otherwise of their stories.

Unfortunately for me, one year before I was due to sit my GCE exams, my father got another job in Sheffield and the family had to move. We found a house in Birdwell, near Barnsley, Yorkshire, which had a view of a large coal tip from the back garden. My parents explained that it had been foggy on the day they decided to buy the house and they had not seen the coal tip! So that I would not have to change schools, I stayed in Loughborough that year and finished as a temporary boarder at the school. I was able to visit my parents at weekends. I still remember the train journey to Sheffield via Iron Cross. I did resent having to stay behind in Loughborough during this period. Being a temporary boarder felt like a prison sentence, although I did continue to have one good friend at the school and more generally got on with many of the students quite well. On Sundays, we all had to attend the local church. I liked some of the hymns and the music but could not identify with the religious worship. I did not like the words of the hymn 'I Vow to Thee, My Country', without being entirely clear why I felt so uneasy about it. Nor could I identify with 'Onward Christian Soldiers', although I quite enjoyed the music. I resented being made to attend church.

I had some adventures during that time. The students were not allowed into Loughborough from the school without permission, but we often broke curfew and visited a coffee bar called El Chico where lots of teenagers and young people went, as well as some older adults. At El Chico, there was often trouble, including fights at times. I remember a small guy headbutting a larger man, resulting in much blood being spilt. I am sure that it was at least partly because of such trouble that the students were usually banned from the town. However, my friend and I continued to be fascinated by the place, partly because of the music on the jukebox but also because the atmosphere seemed so grown up.

On Saturday nights we would go to the cinema, which was allowed. I remember my mate and I watching two early James Bond films when we were underage, and three pretty girls in short miniskirts coming in afterwards and sitting next to us. We were both excited but still far too shy to talk to them. The three girls came in to the El Chico coffee bar the following day and again sat next to us. Two of the girls then left and one remained behind. She then played 'Tired of Waiting' by the Kinks on the jukebox, but nothing else happened. I wished later that I had chatted to her. I think that most regrets in life are usually about what we might have done but did not do.

Anyway, I sat my exams at the end of the school year and got nine O Level GCEs with the top grade in biology and geography, but I only just passed the English language exam. In the geography exam, all of us in the school were lucky that our required study of an Ordnance Survey map was for our area. It certainly made answering questions about topography and places of interest much easier! I was grateful to have finished my brief boarding school period and to be back with my parents and sister in Birdwell. However, we were only there for a further few months before my father was on the move again because of his job – this time to Bracknell in Berkshire.

We lived for a time in a rented modern architect-designed attractive house, with its own small orchard surrounded by a large white brick wall. We were able to rent the property for a limited period, as it was soon to be demolished to make way for a major road being developed as part of the new town. It was by far the most beautiful house we had ever lived in, and yet it was to become associated with much sadness for the family, as my mother was to experience depression and some sort of breakdown while living there. She was admitted for a few months to the Virginia Water sanatorium and was 'treated' with several sessions of electro compulsive therapy (or ECT), a standard treatment at the time. I will always remember the size of the Victorian hospital at Virginia Water, with exceptionally long corridors and large wards. My sister and I did not understand what had happened and my father was unable to explain it to us. We were very worried about our mother and we were so relieved when she was allowed home. Fortunately, she never had to be admitted to hospital again.

However, the new house did have its compensations, especially when my parents and Elaine went away for a few days. A pretty girl that I fancied came to visit with another male friend of mine. We played the new single, 'I Got You Babe', by Sonny and Cher on the gramophone and then had a small party, but unfortunately for me it was my friend who ended up kissing the girl.

My new school was Forest Grammar a few miles away from our home, nearer Reading. I studied economics, geography and history for A Levels, although I had to do the economics O Level GCE exam first. Our teacher of economics and history was a Welshman, who unsurprisingly was very keen on rugby. He provided me, I think, with my first serious intellectual challenges. He used comprehensive notes to teach both history and economics and was usually very thorough and sometimes stimulating in his approach. I remember him saying once in a European nineteenth-century history lesson that 'all men live by their illusions'. I argued with him about how that could be, and instead I spoke in favour of people seeking and living by the 'truth'. I must have appeared to him, like many young people, something of an idealist. Although not always well behaved in his lessons (see below), I learnt a lot from him. I respected him as a teacher.

I certainly did considerable reading in the sixth form. As well as reading the standard texts for all three subjects, I took an option on my own in history to study the French Revolution rather than nineteenth-century British social history. I found this subject fascinating, and it was while I was at the local library searching for relevant books, that I came across, by accident, Eric Hobsbawm's *The Age of Revolution*. The content came to me as a revelation, in terms of its analysis of both the Industrial Revolution and the French Revolution, as well as in its remarkable synthesis of economic, political, social, and cultural history. I was hugely impressed with this book a long time before I began to understand that Hobsbawm, a Marxist, was becoming highly regarded by his peers, students, and those on the left of politics. In fact, he would later be considered by many people as the greatest British historian of his generation. I was later to read many of his books, and his writings had a considerable influence on me. I also enjoyed studying geography, but less so economics. Much of economic theory and analysis seemed vague and uncertain to me, although I did get a grade A in the O Level GCE exam I undertook at the end of my first year in the sixth form.

I soon had a new male friend, Rodger, who studied the same subjects as me and to whom for a period of my youth I was to become close. Although he was very bright, this had not been recognised by the school in his earlier years there, when he had been near the bottom of his form. It was only when he got many A grades at O Level GCE, after he did most of the studying on his own, that the teachers suddenly realised his abilities and potential. We were both outsiders in a way and it seemed natural that we teamed up. Both of us were to do very well academically, but neither of us was to become a prefect in the upper sixth form. Rodger and I sometimes met outside school. I would visit his home and we would talk about books. He had, as well, an interest in classical music and would sometimes play me Sibelius, Shostakovich, and other classical musicians. I was not familiar with such music, so it opened new horizons to me. I also met his father and mother. His father had been an airline pilot but had retired and was retraining to be a teacher. He was interesting to talk to and he would sometimes drive me around in his nice Rover car.

I never really liked the institution of school in terms of its control and rules and I continued to be a rebel. I was soon in serious trouble when I attended a geography field study course in Dale in Pembrokeshire and was discovered with other pupils and girls from another school at night, returning from a clifftop visit where we had shared vodka. Our headmaster threatened us with expulsion but relented. It was because of this event that Rodger and I were never made prefects. On a more trivial level, for some reason, I would read economic books in the history lessons and study history when I was supposed to be learning economics. I would also occasionally truant. I was certainly far from being one of the best behaved pupils.

One initiative by the school during this period that I did appreciate, however, was a sixth-form group that met regularly and informally to discuss broad topics, such as politics or the role of advertising. A young teacher organised the group and as our school was all male, sixth-form girls from the nearby grammar school were also invited. Although still very shy, I very much enjoyed their company. By the end of the sixth form, I had dated two of these girls from the Holt School. The name of my first date was Linda and my second date was Cathy, who would be my girlfriend for the next few years. By the summer of 1967, Cathy and I were spending time with each other regularly. I remember on one occasion the two of us visiting Rodger and showing him to his surprise that we were a couple. Cathy was pretty and talented as an artist but different from me in her view of the world, even though we got on well. When her family had moved to near Reading some time before, she had felt isolated and lonely but had been made welcome by a local church, which she now attended, and she had become very committed to religious worship. Nevertheless, we soon had a close friendship and within a year I was keen to get engaged and was buying a ring. I think I was experiencing adolescent insecurity and wanted the commitment. We did not have a full sexual relationship until I was at university. We were later to live together for several years. Cathy was also to get on very well with my mother.

I recall another pretty girl with blonde hair attending one or two sessions of the young teacher's group, although she was a year younger than the rest of us and in the lower sixth. I never spoke to her at the time because I was too shy, although I was really attracted to her. Our paths were to cross briefly again a couple of years later. Regarding the same group, I also recall that the teacher himself started dating one of the sixth-form girls from Holt School! He would have been in serious trouble with the authorities if he had behaved in more recent times in such a way.

By this time, as you can imagine, I was extremely positive about some of the students at the Holt School for girls. My view was now quite different from when I had first arrived in the area, when the headline in the local paper had reported a fight between girls there, in which bicycle chains and other weapons had been found! From my limited experience, it seemed that Holt School had changed for the better, at least in the sixth form, although of course I was not really in a position to know.

During this period, I started part-time work to ensure I did not just rely on weekly pocket money. I recall with embarrassment that my first Saturday job was at Mac Fisheries, but it only lasted half a day. I spent the time bunging mincemeat into a machine that then produced sausages. I did not like the experience, so at lunchtime, I went home and told my mother that I was not returning! For a while, I then obtained employment at the local supermarket, helping to stack the shelves. It was less messy and a better experience.

In the upper sixth, I applied for university and got an interview with the London School of Economics, having been turned down by Sussex University, which had been my first choice. I was subsequently offered a place, subject to my A Level results, although those interviewing me told me that if they had listened to what my headmaster had said in his reference, no offer would have been forthcoming. Clearly, my headmaster had not forgiven me for what had occurred on the geography field study course! This information about my reference also provided me with an explanation as to why I had been turned down by Sussex University.

Outside of school, I was having an interesting time. I regularly attended a weekly folk club in Wokingham, which I thoroughly enjoyed. As well as traditional folk music, it was there that I was first introduced to protest songs, including those about Lyndon Johnson escalating the Vietnam War. I was certainly to become much more familiar with anti-Vietnam War protests when I attended university.

While at the folk club, I learnt to drink vodka. I remember drinking too much vodka and lime one evening and being put off this combination for life! I also went to London to listen to folk and blues music at a club in Soho called Les Cousins. Sometimes Alexis Korner played. Occasionally, I would stay there for an overnight session. Looking back on it, I am surprised that my parents allowed it. I would have been 17 or 18 years old at the time. While in Soho on one occasion, I also remember chatting to a girl outside a bar where there was a group of young women with lots of makeup on and wearing short skirts. I was rather interested in her, but quite rightly she told me I was too young to come inside the bar with her. Indeed, she then said to me that I should go home. I believe various services were probably on offer on the premises, but I think she had decided to protect me from vice because of my young age! A few months later, just before the football World Cup in 1966 in England, action was taken to clean up Soho by removing prostitutes from the streets in order, supposedly, to protect the many tourists who would be visiting London.

Concerning the drinking of alcohol, I also remember, one Christmas Eve, meeting a group of school friends in Reading and going on a pub crawl and drinking beer, even though we were underage. I must have got very drunk because my next recollection was waking up in bed at home with a terrible hangover. Worse still, the main part of my watch was missing, except for the strap and the glass face. I did recall vaguely walking back the previous night the several miles from Reading to my home, but I had no idea what had happened to my watch! I could not eat my Christmas dinner that day, or any other food. I think I learnt something of a lesson with this incident about excess alcohol and vulnerability, although it certainly did not entirely stop me from future heavy drinking accompanied by sometimes reckless behaviour.

It was also the period of the Beatles' rise to fame. As mentioned above, I started dating Linda from the Holt School and attended a social event at my school with her when 'I Wanna Hold Your Hand' had just come out. We held hands listening to the music as we arrived. I took an interest in the Beatles and bought some of their albums but soon decided that I preferred the music of the Rolling Stones (see below). I also remember kissing Linda and learning that she was wearing stockings and suspenders. It was one of my early erotic experiences.

Additionally, away from school, I was beginning to take some interest in politics. The head boy of the school, whom I liked and got on with, persuaded me to attend one day of the CND (Campaign for Nuclear Disarmament) annual march near Reading on its way to Aldermaston. I was pleased I went with him and found many of the people marching with their banners fascinating. It was undoubtedly my first serious political activity, although during this period, I also remember attending a Young Liberals' wine and cheese party and a Young Socialists' confrontation with the local Conservative MP at a public meeting. I think the attendance at the wine and cheese party probably had more to do with hoping to meet some attractive young women and was not due to any political inclination I may have had at the time.

While mentioning my brief friendship with the head boy of the school, I should explain as well that there was a double tragedy involving two different sixth-form pupils during the period I was there. Firstly, after an evening social event at the school, a sixth former was knocked down and killed by a car at the adjacent main road, with his girlfriend being seriously injured. Secondly, less than a year later, the head boy I already mentioned also died in a car crash while driving, having just passed his driving test. He was just about to go to university. His girlfriend in the car was killed as well. It was the same girl who had been involved in the earlier fatal crash when her previous boyfriend had been killed and she had been injured.

I, like most of my friends, was still doing a part-time job – in my case, it was now working one or two nights, plus Saturdays, in a local corner grocery shop, once again stacking shelves. It was not the most interesting work, but it did at least bring in some extra money. Peter, the owner of the shop, was quite friendly and if nothing else it was further useful work experience. I remember one other girl in the Holt School sixth form, who lived nearby and apparently fancied me, coming into the shop sometimes to say hello. She was pretty but very tall, so as I was only 5 foot 5 inches it would have been difficult for me to date her, so I did not.

Anyway, I got the necessary grades for university and in the autumn of 1967, I was soon commencing my BSc (Econ) honours degree at the London School of Economics. Rodger, my friend from school, also started at LSE at the same time. He had been accepted to study social administration.

I had the last laugh at my disapproving headteacher by winning the school lottery just before my school career ended! I think it almost choked him when he had to present me with the prize at an event in front of all the pupils.

# 3.
# THE STUDENT

Rodger and I shared some accommodation in New Cross during the first year at university, but it was very cold in winter and the following year we both moved to rooms that Rodger had found in a Methodist hostel in Camberwell. Although the study rooms were small, they were comfortable, and breakfast and evening meals were on offer. There were many interesting people living there from different walks of life. I was to get to know a few of them well. There was a student health visitor, the daughter of a famous horror writer and a recovering heroin addict. The pub opposite featured regular music events at weekends, including sometimes an Egyptian belly dancer. The busy East Street market was just up the road. Maybe we would have both been better off initially in our first year living in a university hall of residence, which might have been available, but we had not pursued it. In the medium to longer term, everything worked out well.

As Rodger's girlfriend Jenny had also attended Holt School and was a friend of Cathy, it was natural that we were soon operating as a foursome, although as Cathy had failed to get the necessary grades to attend the Goldsmiths' College art course in London (part of the University of London), she remained at school in our first year to resit the exams. Jenny commenced a psychology course at Goldsmiths' College, which was based in New Cross.

We arrived at LSE at the beginning of the student revolt in the UK, and at the start of the major Vietnam War protests. While studying economics, political thought, British government, international politics and psychology, for exams at the end of the first year, I was soon, therefore, getting a rather different practical political education in student protest and opposition to the Vietnam War. At LSE at the time, there was a significant number of American postgraduate students who had previously been involved in campus protests at Berkeley, Columbia, and elsewhere in the US. Many of these Americans were members of Students for a Democratic Society (SDS). Those that were involved in SDS, along with other students from the Socialist Society, were participating in the wider political struggle in addition to attempting to achieve internal changes to the university. As well as opposing the escalating war in Vietnam, these student leaders were demanding changes in various aspects of wider society. Two favourite chants on student demonstrations were 'Ho, Ho, Ho Chi Minh!' and 'Free, Free, LSE, Free it from the Bourgeoisie!' A small number of these students had also been active in supporting the dock strike in the UK that had been taking place in recent months. One or two students I met at that time also claimed to be anarchists.

One of the substantial issues raised by radical students in my first year was concerns about the appointment of Walter Adams as director of LSE, given his administrative and academic background in apartheid South Africa. This appointment raised issues not only about Dr Adams but also about his selection by the board of governors, which included the controversial chairman, Lord Robbins. Left-wing students were suspicious about and opposed to Walter Adams's appointment and distrusted Lionel Robbins in his role at LSE, as well as disliking him for his liberal market economics. There was also a wider debate taking place about the role of liberal ideology in British universities, involving a critique that suggested that those academics who presented a liberal position on the surface if faced with pressure or a crisis would often resort to a more conservative or even reactionary position defending the status quo and contemporary capitalism.

One interesting issue at the time involved the LSE bookshop, which was basically owned by LSE and overseen by the board of governors chaired by Lord Robbins. As part of the student protests, a significant number of students decided to steal books from the bookshop, read them, and then return them for half-price compensation, allowing resale, thus boosting the students' income. It was a popular practice.

Student militancy at LSE at this time was soon part of a much wider movement involving universities and colleges across the UK. Those attending Colleges of Art were especially prominent in some of the sit-ins and other activities. It should be emphasised, however, that the student protest movement at LSE and elsewhere in the country always, in my experience, involved only a minority (albeit at times a *large* minority) of students. The majority did not partake and continued to focus on their studies.

In my initial period at LSE, there were also to be various memorable events both there and away from it. First, this was a period soon after Enoch Powell, the Conservative politician, had made his infamous speech predicting future 'rivers of blood' as a consequence of mass immigration. Some London dockers, led by Jack Dash, decided to support him, and they arranged a demonstration at Westminster outside Parliament. There was also a counterdemonstration with many students present, which I attended. Following various chanting by both groups, the dockers on one side of the road decided they were going to demonstrate their support for Powell by breaking through the police lines, running across the road, and attacking those demonstrating against them. The policing was inadequate and fighting soon broke out. Not being very skilful in this area, I was soon punched in the face by a small but seemingly strong opponent who had more boxing skills than I did! With a badly bruised face, I had some explaining to do when I next met my tutor at LSE.

Secondly, and most memorably, after the events of May 1968, the BBC decided to make a TV programme about the worldwide student revolt and paid for various student leaders to travel to London. These students were soon speaking in the Old Theatre at the LSE, describing their various struggles (especially regarding opposition to the Vietnam War), and I was in the audience listening to them. The lecture theatre was packed out and overflowing as we listened to Daniel Cohn-Bendit, a student leader from the University of Nanterre and the Sorbonne, involved in the May events taking place in Paris, SDS students from Germany, Japanese students, American students, Czech students involved in the Prague Spring, and many others. It certainly felt like a worldwide movement and was both intensely exciting and very empowering, even though many different views and perspectives were forthcoming from socialists, communists, Maoists and anarchists. Undoubtedly, the most poignant speech was from a Czech student experiencing the Prague Spring, who emphasised their struggle for basic rights such as freedom of speech, which he noted many of the others present took for granted. Overall, it was almost possible to believe that the world really could be changed in major ways for the better and that perhaps capitalism was not all-powerful. One suggestion was for the development of red bases, which would then build links with the working class. Although we were certainly naive in some respects about how change could be achieved particularly regarding the possibility of the engagement of the working class, my involvement in these events means that even today I believe that with the mobilisation of enough support, radical progressive change is still possible.

Thirdly, because of a previous protest and sit-in, the authorities at LSE had somewhat unwisely decided, by early 1969, to install security gates in various areas, which could be closed if there was trouble. I think the idea was to prevent any full occupation of the buildings. Unsurprisingly, the militant section of the student body could not accept this new reality and decided to take direct action. I watched as an axe was taken to what proved to be rather flimsy gates. They were all removed within a short time and they were never to be introduced again. However, there were other repercussions which included the LSE administration using Court injunctions to ban certain students from any further activities. I recall that Dr Paul Hoch, an American postgraduate student who was undertaking a post-doctoral thesis on the philosophy of mathematics, appearing in the High Court in the Strand, representing himself. I attended one day of the hearing.

The Vietnam War was my war in much the same way as the Second World War belonged to the previous generation. It created a political catalyst that led many young, and some older, people not only to oppose the war the Americans were fighting against a small developing country in Southeast Asia in the name of anti-communism, but to question the nature of capitalism itself. It was obvious to us that the Vietnamese government and people, rather than being part of some international communist conspiracy, had instead been fighting what was essentially a nationalist struggle against colonialism and imperialism since the Second World War. In fact, the Vietnam War radicalised large numbers of people worldwide and became a key moral issue that divided opinion, especially in the United States, and led to the questioning of the status quo and the post-Second World War orthodoxy arising from the Cold War.

The domino theory on Communist conspiracy was fatally undermined by the Americans waging a war against a people who rather than being controlled by the Chinese had been struggling for their independence against them for at least a thousand years. The dreadful television and camera images of the bombing and destruction, with the widespread use of napalm, in a military campaign carried out indiscriminately against civilians as well as the Vietnamese guerrillas, raised crucial moral as well as political questions. It was only much later that I was to read books on the war, including Neil Sheehan's *A Bright Shining Lie*, quite recently, Christian Appy's collection of interviews, and Ken Burns and Geoffrey Ward's book (following their impressive television series), which have highlighted the dreadful nature of what happened, the lies that were told by the American political and military establishment, and their collusion with corrupt and self-serving successive South Vietnamese governments. For me, these excellent books and the television commentary have only validated further the views I had held all along.

Early on at LSE, I did attend various major demonstrations in London to protest against the Vietnam War, although for some reason I was not at the most famous, and for some people notorious, one that took place at Grosvenor Square. I can recall the huge turnouts, the array of flags, including trade union banners and those of the socialists, communists, Maoists and anarchists, as well as the excitement and on occasion also the violence between the police and some demonstrators. My politics were certainly evolving during this period and I was becoming more radical. At the beginning, I attended, rather naively, an American student protest that listed all the recent American deaths in Vietnam and wondered why these protestors were being barracked by the LSE Socialist Society. Later, I was to understand much better of course that the main victims in Vietnam were the Vietnamese and, of course, not the Americans. Any remembrance event that just listed the American deaths (which would eventually reach a total of more than 50,000) but not the Vietnamese fatalities, both soldiers and civilians who died in their millions, would always be a travesty.

It was during this time of student protests at the London School of Economics that I attended a fundraising concert for the students, given by The Who at the Roundhouse in North London. They were excellent and I will always remember bobbing up and down to their music after a few drinks and thoroughly enjoying it. Later, while I was still a student, one of the most memorable of such music events for me (but for a different reason) was attending the Isle of Wight Festival with some friends, at which Bob Dylan was performing. Along with many other thousands of fans, we returned extremely disappointed when he finished after only 50 minutes and without playing many of his most popular protest songs. I should add that my favourite rock group continued to be at this time The Rolling Stones. I was appreciative of their attachment to the American blues tradition as well as more mainstream rock 'n' roll. I liked all their music in preference to The Beatles, who seemed to me to be more conformist – although lots of parents and older people would have disagreed!

In between these protests, I did however still manage to study some economics, political thought, and international politics, although I also spent time becoming more familiar with other subjects rather than those I was supposed to be concentrating on. I had realised by this stage that my choice of international relations, as a main subject, had probably been a mistake. It was becoming clear to me that sociology would have been a better choice. One vivid memory is that of attending the young lecturer Robin Blackburn's seminars on the 'Sociology of Revolution', which included a focus on contemporary Russian, Chinese and Cuban societies. He had returned recently from Cuba where he had met Fidel Castro and was keen to tell us about what Fidel had said and to explain various aspects of the Cuban Revolution. I was fascinated and learnt quite a lot. I was also soon reading the *New Left Review* periodical and other Left-leading literature. I became familiar with some of the classical texts of Marxism, including the *Communist Manifesto* and Lenin's *State and Revolution*.

Of course, some of the militancy at LSE gradually subsided, although large protests against the Vietnam War continued into 1970 and beyond. These various student experiences though had certainly helped to develop my political views. I had developed a socialist perspective but one with a libertarian outlook. I was both anti-capitalist and anti-Stalinist. A more equal society had to be the goal.

In my second year at LSE, I continued to be involved in protests but also undertook at least some relevant studying. My work included writing a long essay on the causes of Fascism, which my tutor rated highly and circulated to some of his postgraduate students. An understanding of the causes of Fascism and the Second World War was especially important to me and in writing this long essay I believe I had made considerable progress in getting to know the key factors and the dynamics that had led to such a terrible period in European history. The most important building blocks for the rise of Fascism were the economic crises in the 1920s, which destroyed the livelihoods of the German lower middle class and many others, the force of nationalism fuelled by the perceived humiliation of the Treaty of Versailles, and the fear of communism and the left.

I was well served during this period by the libraries I was able to use. As well as the LSE British Library of Economics and Political Science, and the LSE student library, I had access to the University of London library and the Goldsmiths' College library because of the links with Cathy and Jenny. I was later to use, memorably, on one occasion, with a temporary research card, the famous round British Library Reading Room, in which Karl Marx had regularly studied when writing *Das Kapital*. I was certainly excited being there as I reflected on the fact that he had undertaken so much of his research sitting in this place so many years ago. The British Library was later moved to Euston, North London.

During this period as a student, I still found time to read more widely, especially some European literature. My favourite writer was Fyodor Dostoevsky, who then and still now I regard as a genius because of his brilliant dialogism and psychological insight into human behaviour. The first novel I read was *Crime and*

*Punishment* and I was soon to appreciate all his great novels and much of his other writing, including *Notes from the Underground*. They had an important emotional as well as intellectual influence on me, which is hard to explain. Even when he disagreed strongly with the views and behaviour of many of his characters, he presented their arguments in a clear and cogent way as well as describing what he considered their emotional motivation for their various behaviours. Moreover, while his approach is always grounded in the social circumstances of nineteenth-century Russia, like all great writers, his work provides great insights into the wider human condition. Although his religious and political beliefs linked to his Slavophile views are always apparent in his novels, they do not distract from his genius. Unsurprisingly, it was Einstein who said that he learnt more from Dostoevsky than anyone else, including all the great scientists. I also became fascinated with his life, including his mock execution ordered by the Czar for his links to those liberals and progressives who wanted to modernise Russia, his exile in Siberia, and his gambling addiction (see the later chapter on my heroes).

During the summer holidays while I was at university, I worked as a conductor for several years on the local buses in Berkshire. It was great fun at the time and I still look back on it with fond memories. I worked in an area bordered by Reading, Camberley and Windsor. It provided a good opportunity for meeting young women and I did have a few dates with one young lady who worked as an assistant to a local optician. I also recall meeting again the pretty blonde girl from Holt School who had attended one session of our sixth form group. She got on the bus at Reading and sat near to where

I was standing. It seemed that she was interested in at least talking to me. Unfortunately, I was much too shy and we hardly exchanged a word. Looking back, it was certainly a missed opportunity! I should add that during the summer period when I had dates with the optician's assistant, I had fallen out with my girlfriend Cathy, although we were back together again soon after I returned to university.

Most passengers, when I was a conductor, were pleasant enough, although one or two people did try to avoid paying the full fare by offering you half of it and telling you to keep the money without you issuing them a ticket. However, transporting many of the school children on 'specials' was a less pleasant experience, as they often misbehaved. It was difficult to say who was naughtier, the girls or the boys. I got on well with the drivers and other conductors, whom I spent time with either on the road or in the canteen. I also recall with sadness the behaviour of one of the drivers who always seemed to spend hours after receiving his pay packet on a Friday night on the slot machine in the canteen. He would regularly lose a lot or most of his pay packet while on this dreadful machine. On reflection, I am surprised that no one was able to stop him from losing his money in this way.

In my final year at university, I concentrated more on my books and finished up, perhaps a little surprisingly after the first two years, with a more than acceptable upper second honours degree. I got a first-class score on my main paper on international politics but did less well on some of the other subjects. I would soon be joining the world of work.

My parents were of course more than pleased that I got my degree but were disappointed that I decided not to attend the degree ceremony. My father, as a *Daily Express* reader, could not comprehend my attitude and left-wing politics. He had wanted me to be a barrister, which was not going to happen. He was later to say after we argued regularly about politics that 'if I was a Communist, I should go and live in the Soviet Union'. I then had to explain that I was extremely critical of the Soviet Government as well as aspects of our own society. Indeed, I knew that if I had been living in Russia after the Revolution, I would probably have finished in the Gulag or with a bullet in the back of my head. However, on reflection, I think that all these political arguments were a substitute for any emotional interaction or closeness. Sadly, neither of us was able to articulate in any clear way our feelings and frustrations regarding our unsatisfactory relationship or at least explain to each other our mutual desire to better understand each other. I do not think it was anybody's fault but just the way it happened, given the nature of my father's upbringing, his life experience, and the way Elaine and I had been brought up. My mother had not been able to significantly modify such experiences, despite her greater emotional responsiveness, given my father's dominance and my mother's own nervous personality.

# 4.
# YOUNG FRIENDSHIPS

As mentioned earlier, Cathy was my girlfriend during these years. After she had retaken her exams during my first year at LSE, she was offered a place at Goldsmiths' College to study art, so there were soon four friends, Rodger, Jenny, Cathy and myself, with two of us studying at London School of Economics and two at Goldsmiths' College, Camberwell, which was also part of London University. We were often in each other's company. As I mentioned above, Rodger and I had moved in our second year at LSE to live in a Methodist hostel in Camberwell.

Cathy and I met another Roger there, a trainee accountant from Bradford, who was also to become a good friend. When he qualified, he moved to a flat in Hampstead and Cathy and I would regularly visit him there on a Friday night and have a few beers in The Flask pub and later in the evening a curry in Belsize Park. On my twenty-first birthday, he treated both of us to a meal at the top of the newly opened Post Office Tower. The restaurant rotated 360 degrees during your meal, so you got a spectacular view of the London skyline. It was to be shut down in the 1970s because of the terrorist threat from the IRA. We also went on trips with him to his family home in Baildon, West Yorkshire. Once qualified, he bought a Triumph sportscar and I had several journeys with him up and down the newly extended M1. Later, he was to move to Canada, and in the mid-1970s I would travel once to his home in Burlington, by Lake Ontario, near Toronto, using a Laker Airways cheap flight from London to New York and one of the famous Greyhound coaches to travel from there to Toronto. I saw little of New York beyond Times Square, as I only spent one night there. Rodger had already bought a yacht and I accompanied him on one occasion when he was taking part in a race. It was quite an experience yacht-racing on Lake Ontario. I also recall having one or two wonderful seafood meals there. I did visit Niagara Falls on the way back to New York and then home. Sadly, we were not to maintain contact in later life. Rodger did phone me more than 10 years later when I was living in Nottingham (having obtained my phone number from Nottinghamshire County Council's personnel section) to invite me to a party in Baildon, Yorkshire, as he was back in the UK for a holiday while still living in the United States with his wife and family. It was at a time when, for various reasons (see below), I was feeling low and declined to go. I have in recent years very much regretted that decision.

While living in the hostel and waiting to meet Cathy outside the Elephant and Castle underground station, I remember one unfortunate incident when a middle-aged drunk came up to me and punched me in the face without saying a word. He then wandered off. I wondered then and still wonder now if there was any reason why he had taken a dislike to me. Probably not. I had something of a black eye but otherwise was alright! It was the second time I had been punched in the face while at university following the earlier incident outside Parliament at the dockers' demonstration supporting Enoch Powell.

Unfortunately, also in my second year at university, the other Rodger, who had been doing well in his studying of social administration at LSE, had a serious car accident while on a trip to Hereford. As a result of this, he had serious injuries to his leg and was in hospital there for several weeks. I hitch-hiked to see him at Hereford and found him in quite good spirits, although it was clear that he had experienced a lot of pain. In retrospect, it was to become apparent that this experience had somehow changed his view of the world and to some extent his personality. He soon stopped studying and within a short space of time, he had left university and was seeking employment. He also began to experiment with drugs. We were still friends but never quite so close again. Rodger and Jenny were soon to separate, so the quartet, in effect, disappeared.

The hitch-hiking experience back to London from Hereford was also an interesting one. I was picked up not far from the hospital by a young man who told me he was training to be a vet and said he could take me all the way back to London. He then drove me for the next three hours at high speed and in ways that, in my view, were extremely dangerous. He seemed to ignore all the usual road hazards and assumed that everyone else would take the necessary avoiding action. It was a very scary experience, especially when he told me that he was not expecting to live a long life and that he wanted to have an exciting time while he was still about! Fortunately for me, we got to London without any accidents or other problems. He invited me to a future party, but I did not attend.

Later on, after I had graduated, I was involved in a serious car accident on the M1 motorway when Cathy and I were going to a party in Bradford arranged by our friend Roger, the accountant whom I mentioned above. We were in the back seats of a hire car driven by an Australian woman friend, only a few miles north of London, when she lost control of the vehicle and it spun round several times across the carriageway, central area and the other carriageway before finishing up facing the wrong way on the hard shoulder on the opposite side of the road. At that time there was no central barrier to stop this happening. As it was a Friday night, and the road was extremely busy, we were undoubtedly lucky that no other car hit us and were not therefore killed or seriously injured. The police told us that when such an accident took place on the motorway, they sometimes had to "scrape people off the road". This observation did not make us feel any better.

While I was still studying, Cathy joined me living in the Methodist hostel in Camberwell when she started the arts course at Goldsmiths' College, but after I graduated, we were soon sharing a flat in Crouch End, North London. I was to live there in the attic flat for nine years. In Crouch End at that time, there was an interesting mixture of people: some students, some hippies, and some working-class and more middle-class people. The Queens Head pub provided a meeting place as well as a drinking venue for many of us. There were lots of drugs being used, but we did not participate, except once or twice when I experimented with cannabis. As I did not smoke tobacco, I remember having some cannabis in a chocolate cake without any major effect. I did also try an amphetamine on one occasion when we went to a party. It gave me a high, but when I came down, I was incredibly tired for more than 24 hours. I did not try it again. Tariq Ali, at that time still a revolutionary, lived just up the road.

When I first moved to Crouch End, I maintained contact for a while with my friend Rodger who had attended the sixth form at Forest Grammar School and then London School of Economics (before he'd dropped out in our second year as I mentioned above). However, it was becoming clear that we were growing apart for various reasons, including his drug taking. We were soon to lose contact with each other. Later, I did arrange to meet his ex-girlfriend Jenny once at my flat and went out for a drink with her. She was doing well and had become a lecturer in social work. It felt strange, however, being together and not being part of a foursome with Rodger and Cathy. After that visit, we were also to lose contact with each other.

# 5.
# THE POLITICAL ACTIVIST

My political views had evolved throughout my three years at university and I remained a socialist and both anti-imperialist and anti-capitalist. I believed that while colonialism was almost at an end economic imperialism by the United States and other Western countries remained a dominant force in the world economy. I also believed that capitalism had to be substantially modified and controlled by a reformed social state that served most people and did not operate in the interests of the small minority who still owned most of the capital. I also considered at this time the Soviet Union to be a 'degenerated workers' state' and therefore I had some affinity with the various Trotskyist groups who opposed both the Communist Party and the Labour Party. Theoretically, I considered myself closer to the International Marxist Group (IMG) but regarding practical activity favoured more the International Socialists (IS) who at least were engaged in a considerable amount of trade union activity. I eventually joined the International Socialists.

My involvement with the International Socialists (soon to become the Socialist Workers Party) was to last for several years and I did attend innumerable meetings and a lot of demonstrations. As a party member, you were required to show such commitment, including taking an active part as mentioned above in the appropriate trade union. In my case, this was NALGO and I was soon an active branch member as well as one of the representatives to the Metropolitan District.

The organisation had only a small core of dedicated members, including Tony Cliff, the main theoretician who (as a Trotskyist) had written a key book on Russia being 'state capitalist', but the Party also had a much larger group of followers. I was soon to learn that there was a high turnover of these comrades. Anyway, I found myself disagreeing with aspects of the 'state capitalist' analysis and soon recognised that I had more affinity with the IMG analysis of Russia. In this respect, I was very much influenced by Isaac Deutscher's work, especially *The Unfinished Revolution*, as well as his monumental biography on Leon Trotsky. Looking back now, I think I probably should have accepted more readily the 'state capitalist' analysis.

I was also involved at this time in the anti-racist struggle, as the National Front was selling newspapers in the East End of London and arranging some demonstrations. The newly named Socialist Workers Party was then involved with others in the Rock Against Racism movement, which was very successful for a period in mobilising young people against the activities of the National Front. I recall attending one popular concert in Victoria Park. The fascists and racists of the National Front also tried to hold meetings in various parts of the East End, as they believed that a significant part of the population might be sympathetic to their cause, considering that many new immigrants (mainly Bangladeshi) had been moving into East London. On one occasion, John Tyndall, leader of the National Front, had been allowed to hire a local school for a meeting, to the disgust of at least some local people. I was involved with SWP members, and others, in entering the school and breaking up the meeting so that Tyndall and others could not spread their poison.

After an initial period of this political activity, my enthusiasm began to wane, and on one occasion at least, I had other branch members call at my flat, asking me why I had not attended the last meeting. It seemed to me that the wide range of activities in many areas produced meagre results and I was to resign my membership in the mid-1970s. I was becoming even less convinced by the political analysis on offer, as I was increasingly viewing the world in shades of grey rather than as black and white. I think I would have found it difficult to toe any party line.

Beyond political literature, I was still reading a lot. I took a special interest in existentialism, especially the post-Second World War work of Jean-Paul Sartre and Albert Camus. I very much liked Sartre's series of novels, '*The Roads to Freedom*', and Camus' *The Outsider* and *The Plague*. It also led me to some wider interest in French literature and other aspects of French intellectual life.

# 6.
# THE SOCIAL WORKER

When I graduated from London School of Economics in 1970, I was soon looking for a job. As on principle I excluded seeking work in the financial sector or being employed by large corporations in general, I found myself more attracted towards health and social care. The Seebohm reorganisation of 1971 offered opportunities and I was soon an assistant childcare officer in the east of London. My area team covered areas adjacent to the River Thames. A few months later I was an assistant social worker following the reorganisation and within a year an unqualified social worker.

At the age of 22, and without any training but a brief induction, I began supporting children and families in an area which at the time was one of the most deprived in London, albeit not that far from the City of London with its tower blocks and vast wealth. I was very much thrown in the deep end and I was soon allocated various cases transferred from two very experienced social workers in the team. Looking back on what happened from my perspective now, it was obviously inappropriate that I was placed in this situation without sufficient training and closer supervision.

One of the first cases I was given involved a family, in which the father had recently attacked the previous female social worker, having put his hands round her neck and held her over a balcony. He had been brought up in care in Ireland and had serious mental health problems. He was an alcoholic and could be very violent to members of his own family and others when he had been drinking. Perhaps surprisingly he still worked in a local brewery! He would sometimes attack his wife and he also abused his sons frequently once they were approaching adolescence. Although I developed a good working relationship with the family, over several years there were occasions when he was aggressive to me as well as to his wife and children, including one serious incident when his wife left him for a period, and in a drunken stupor he threatened me with a chisel by waving it in my face. We had also taken a decision at that time to take one of the boys into care after he had been beaten by his father. Another of the boys, who seemed very disturbed, was already in care in a specialist boarding school for children with learning disabilities. There were also several young girls in the family, but for whatever reason they seemed to fare better and there was less concern about their welfare.

Another of my initial cases involved a 14-year-old boy who had been placed on a care order following convictions for burglaries and criminal damage. He was also not attending school. His father was a somewhat unsuccessful bank robber with mental health difficulties who had been to prison several times. He still seemed to expect his children to obey the law while his mother appeared to be worn down by her responsibilities and the care of the three children. We placed the teenager in a local children's home that was an assessment centre with a small education unit attached. He was soon making significant progress in terms of his behaviour and his attendance at the local specialised education unit. Although a psychiatrist, as part of the assessment process, recommended that he should be sent to a distant community home with education (what would have previously been called an approved school), I managed to persuade other members attending his planning meeting that he should remain for a period at his current children's home and continue to attend the education unit. It worked well and he finished his schooling there. We subsequently discharged him home and he managed to get a job as an assistant working on a van. He developed a good working relationship with me to the extent that on one occasion, not at my request, he travelled several miles from his home to see me with some of his mates. He made considerable progress during his adolescence in terms of moving away from offending in the period I knew him. I also recall taking him, while he was in care, to see a football match in West London where my team, Nottingham Forest, was playing Chelsea. It was a boring 0–0 draw. As he was a Millwall supporter, I do not think he was much impressed by this experience!

One other bit of information about him sticks in my mind. Although many people would have described him as a 'juvenile delinquent' and therefore labelled him with regard to how they would have expected him to behave, on Sundays, he would go horse riding with some of his mates in Redbridge. I learnt from such experiences to be careful about how certain stigmatising labels are applied to youngsters, as they often obscure the full picture.

I also dealt with another of his mates who had been in trouble with the police for theft and burglaries. He was made the subject of a care order and placed in a community home with education (CHE) in Essex. I remember visiting him there, where he showed me a well that seemed important to him. It had been dug by his father who had been to the same institution many years ago. He did well at the CHE and before long we brought him home. While I was supervising him, he did not offend again.

Another case involved a black adolescent boy of Caribbean origin. Again, when I first met him, he had been placed in a CHE some time ago. The staff there considered that he had made substantial progress and I was able to implement a plan for him to return home. This action was successful and he did not re-offend in the period that I knew him. I remember years later bumping into him on a Nottingham street when he was with some of his mates. I said hello to him, and I heard him saying under his breath to his friends who had been looking at me that 'I was alright'.

A fifth case involved a family in which all the teenage boys except one were in serious trouble with the police for burglary, car theft and similar offences. The magistrates at the juvenile courts knew them well and I sometimes felt they were being punished for their family name rather than for the offence they had been charged with. I remember talking to one of the boys in the cells after he had been sent to a detention centre and I recall him stating that I seemed to be much more upset than he was about what had happened. I just felt that his offence did not merit such a sentence. Perhaps surprisingly, the teenager in the family that I was most worried about was the one who had been convicted of no offences. I was concerned about him because I had once seen him lose control completely with another boy whom he had punched repeatedly. In fact, it was this teenager who subsequently was involved in various violent offences later in his life. In comparison, his siblings soon left crime behind them and led less antisocial lives. In some areas in the east of London, you always had to remember that in the 1970s, one third of all boys had appeared in juvenile court by the age of 14.

My workload included child protection cases both in terms of preventing neglect and abuse as well as also dealing with children already admitted to care for these reasons. I remember visiting a young girl in a small residential home who was no more than four or five years old and asking her about the mark or scar on her chest. There was an open coal fire in the room and without hesitation, she approached it and picked up the poker. She then indicated to me that was how her mark had been caused. Fortunately, of course, she was at least by then in a safe environment.

I also dealt with another family whose little boy was admitted to hospital having suffered significant damage to his pelvis, which the doctor treating him considered to be consistent with him having been forcibly kicked. He was initially admitted into care for further assessment. I worked with the boy (perhaps 8 years old) and the family. The boy and his parents all claimed an accident had occurred and he had injured himself falling on to some furniture. The parents were immature but seemingly very caring about their son, who wanted to return home. Considering that there was some doubt about the cause of the injury, a case conference later agreed that he should be returned home under supervision, although it was understood that were some risks in carrying out this course of action. I continued to supervise the family for some considerable time. The following Christmas, I got a card from them stating 'Peace within this House'.

Other child protection cases I was involved with required my seeking legal advice and applying to the Court for interim or full care orders. I recall having to take such action with one family where I had been supervising them at home for some time but where there was increasing evidence of neglect. I had to give evidence in court justifying our application. It was necessary but difficult as the mother had probably come to regard me more as a supportive friend than a social worker.

Another tragic case involved a family of six children in care who were all together in a large children's home. Their mother had disappeared, but at least their father, who had his own serious problems, visited them regularly at least once a month. His nickname was Lucky and I could see he was doing his best to keep in contact with the children. However, I was informed one day that he had been killed in a car crash. I felt terribly sad for the children and had the awful but essential task of having to inform them all about what happened. I still wonder today what happened to them in later life. I pleaded with my managers that we should pay for a headstone for his burial, but the money was not forthcoming.

As we had generic caseloads of childcare, older people and people with mental health difficulties, I was also allocated a case involving an intelligent, attractive woman in her late twenties who had bipolar disorder. For whatever reason, she had been allocated a flat on the top floor of a tower block. I got on well with her and I think was quite effective in providing her with support, but one day the director of social services received a long rambling letter from her about me, which seemed to suggest that our relationship had moved on from being professional. It was not true, but I had to see the director and explain to him in some considerable detail what had been happening. On another occasion when she saw me, she told me that a woman downstairs in her block of flats was having problems and she requested that I see her. I agreed to go downstairs and meet her. She was quite an attractive married woman, who proceeded to somewhat embarrass me by telling me that she was having problems with her husband because he was not a 'real man'. By the way she expressed herself, and by showing me a lot of her legs, I had no doubt that I was being invited to help her out in overcoming these difficulties! I hurriedly offered to refer her to our social work intake team and took leave of her rather rapidly.

I also had to supervise one or two elderly people living on their own who were at risk of neglect but who had rejected any help in providing services such as home helps or meals on wheels. I remember one elderly man who had consistently refused social workers access in the past. After several visits, I did manage to get him to allow me in. The inside of the flat was in a poor state with rubbish scattered about, but on the other hand, he did seem okay in terms of his physical and mental health, to the extent I could assess him. Again, he refused any services, seemingly valuing his independence too much. I felt that all I could do was to try and monitor the situation, knowing that if there became much greater concern about his physical health and the conditions he was living in, as a last resort, legal powers for access and the cleansing of his property could be taken under the National Assistance Act 1948. Alternatively, if his mental health deteriorated, action might be taken for a compulsory admission to hospital under the Mental Health Act 1959. While gaining access continued to be difficult, my assessment was that I did not need to resort to any of these powers in the period that I supervised him.

We had sometimes to carry out assessments on individuals and families who contacted us stating they were homeless and requesting temporary or permanent accommodation. On one occasion, I interviewed this pretty young woman in a see-through blouse that showed her bra, who claimed to be homeless, so as usual I went to visit her where she had informed me she had been staying. It was only a small room with a large bed in it, and as I talked to her from the opposite side of the bed, I felt something grab my leg. It was an Alsatian dog that had been hiding under the bed, and it was soon being hit by a man with a big stick who emerged from another room. The woman was very apologetic, as I had to go to hospital for some stitches and an injection against tetanus, but it seemed likely to me that she was probably using the existing room for the purpose of prostitution and that the man with the big stick was probably her pimp. We did not provide any accommodation.

Our team, as mentioned above, was responsible for mental health assessments, including consideration of compulsory admissions. We all held a warrant card, being mental health officers. It was often one of the most difficult areas of work. I recall on one occasion being called to assess an actor who was working in a small local theatre. He had been pestering other female actors in the belief that he was God and it was their duty to serve him. When I met him, there were indications that he was somewhat manic, but on the other hand, he was quite lucid and reasonable. At the time, I did not feel there were grounds for a compulsory admission and he declined any immediate voluntary treatment. Unfortunately, 72 hours later, he had climbed up onto a roof in Central London and was subsequently detained by the police and soon after admitted for assessment to a mental health hospital.

After a couple of years, our area team was divided into two smaller teams to better deal with the workload. I joined the intake team. We would undertake initial assessments and short-term work, including welfare rights and debt management assistance. If work required longer-term intervention, it would be transferred to the other team. Our senior social worker was an interesting character who had previously been a merchant seaman. We also had community workers operating from the same base. The members of the intake team worked very well together and we developed some expertise in areas such as welfare rights and housing matters. As there was an increasingly large Bangladeshi community in the area, we were also involved in some outreach work to facilitate better access to services for these new immigrants. I do recall that on one occasion when I was with a Bangladeshi man who was requesting help in getting rehoused, that at the end of the interview, he put some money on the table. Obviously, his experience in Bangladesh had been that if you wanted some service from local officials in that country, you had to bribe them.

Team members also socialised with each other. We would regularly be in the pub next to the office after work. I also had contact with many other interesting people in the east of London, including Dan, who was both a local detached youth worker and a well-known artist.

I remained in the intake team for three more years before I went back to London School of Economics to undertake my social work qualification. At my leaving do, Dan gave me two signed prints of his paintings. I should also mention that towards the end of this period, in February 1975, I had another narrow escape when travelling as usual on the Northern City underground line between Highbury and Moorgate stations. A terrible crash occurred at Moorgate a few minutes after

I usually travelled, with 43 people being killed and many being injured. As usual, I had sat in the front carriage that morning and it was in that carriage that most people had died when the train failed to stop as it reached Moorgate station. I was both very distressed at what happened but, of course, very relieved that I had not been on that train.

The social work course was notable mainly for the other students I met, including a very bright German guy who because of his academic brilliance in Heidelberg had been allowed to use Hegel's old study. Another intelligent woman on the course was the partner of a consultant psychiatrist whom I got to know quite well while working in the East End. Many of us soon connected in opposing the theoretical approach to social work advocated by our tutor, who was a Freudian. The narrowness of this approach was apparent to most of us, as we were more interested in practical support, behavioural approaches and community activities rather than traditional therapeutic social work. After some discussions between those students concerned and our female tutor, she stood down and we managed our own tutorials for the rest of the course.

It was during this period that Mandy, my girlfriend at the time, died of a drug overdose (see below). I then had the strange experience of studying loss and bereavement when I was trying to come to terms with it in my own life. I was very raw emotionally and felt I was struggling to prepare for my exams and a short dissertation and get to the end of my course, which was under three months away. Somehow, I managed to do it with some support from friends, although I recall being up all night completing the dissertation the day before I had to hand it in. I wrote about systems theory and how biological theories had been transferred to social science and social work with both positive and negative consequences. In fact, my emotional distress did not seem to do me any harm in terms of academic performance, as I got a distinction for one written exam (out of two) and also for my dissertation. However, I believe I did less well on my poorly chosen placement in a child guidance clinic where the two psychiatrists differed in their theoretical approaches – one was Freudian and the other Jungian. A better choice of placement for me would have been community work.

Soon afterwards, I was back as a qualified social worker working in another area, and within only six months, I had been promoted to a senior social worker there. Somewhat surprisingly, for a post that was not on a senior manager grade, my selection panel consisted of local councillors. I got on well with the area director and other members of the team, but it was not an ideal situation and the work pressures were considerable.

Regarding social work activities, I recall that soon after I started in the new location, I was allocated a teenage girl to deal with who was in some trouble with the police for taking and driving away vehicles with her boyfriend. I can recall how attractive she appeared and, no doubt inappropriately, I was soon characterising her and her boyfriend as 'Bonnie and Clyde'. She had been placed by the juvenile court under a supervision order and fortunately, during the period I supervised her, she was not to offend again.

I was responsible for quite a mixed team of social workers, who varied a lot in their experience, including an older woman, a female nun, an older man, and a young social work assistant. Most members of the team specialised in childcare, although the older man had been a member of the old Welfare Department before 1970 and worked entirely with elderly people. In childcare, we had the usual mixture of child protection work and support and supervision of teenagers in various kinds of difficulties, including behavioural problems and offending. While supervising them, I learnt a lot in quite a short period of time. The nun was very experienced and a skilful and capable worker. The older woman lacked confidence but was very conscientious and supportive of her clients. The older man was also very experienced in dealing with a wide range of issues involving the elderly. The social work assistant was very motivated, eager to learn and a hard worker.

It was soon after I was promoted that a bizarre event occurred, which resulted in an assistant social worker from another area team being placed with me for a temporary period. He had been driving when he had been forced to swerve to avoid running down a dog that had crossed in front of him. He had just caught the dog on the side of his bonnet and had got out of his car to see if it was alright. A woman who had been with the dog, though, was agitated, and she had told him that her partner would be angry and that he should leave straight away. As she spoke to him she looked back to some flats, and as he followed her gaze he saw a man running down the stairs with an axe in his hand. Unsurprisingly, he jumped back in the car to try to get away but then panicked as he turned the ignition and stalled the car. As he managed on second attempt to start the car and begin to move away, the man who was now running down the street reached the car and buried the axe in the boot. Our assistant social worker got away, but only just! No wonder he needed a temporary transfer to our area and some support to help him recover from this trauma.

In the mid to late 1970s, I continued to live in the same flat in Crouch End. By this time, I had not been living with Cathy for a while (see below). I had two flatmates downstairs, initially two guys, one of whom was Phil; I would often socialise with him. He was a civil servant and a Manchester City football supporter. Later, two Australian girls lived there for a while. Again, I got on well with them to the extent I remember one girl coming back from a night out and uninvited jumping into bed with me as I had already gone to sleep. I can report that nothing happened!

It was during this period that an unusual and rather funny incident occurred one Christmas when I went to stay with my parents, who were then renting on a short-stay basis a flat in Victoria, not far from Buckingham Palace. Elaine, my sister, was there for Christmas as well and had brought her cat. On Christmas Day, we all decided to go for a walk in nearby St James's Park, with the cat on a long lead. Unfortunately, a dog attacked the cat and somehow the cat got off the lead, ran away and then climbed a tree. Despite lots of coaxing, the cat, who was obviously scared by what had happened, then refused to come down from the tree. My father finished up phoning the fire brigade, who unsurprisingly were not keen on Christmas Day to come out and rescue the cat. Instead, we spotted a builder's yard with a ladder in it, which we then borrowed for our rescue operation. I remember walking past Buckingham Palace holding the ladder. My father then went up the tree on the ladder and rescued the cat, although it did claw him and draw some blood before the operation was successful!

In the late 1970s, I also decided to do some more studying. As Professor Jock Young, one of the main academics developing the 'New Criminology' course, taught at Middlesex Polytechnic, I enrolled for night classes there on the 'Sociology of Deviancy'. I found it very interesting and read some of the main books they had produced. Jock Young was quite a charismatic teacher. However, as far as I was concerned, the star of the show was Mike McKenna, who lectured on 'Methods and Models: Philosophy of Science'. He provided a brilliant critical overview of the development of European philosophy, including the significance of Kant and Hegel. Unfortunately, he was also an alcoholic and I remember him attempting to give one lecture very inebriated with a beer glass in one hand. He was unable to speak more than a few slurred words before leaving the class. I gave up the course at the end of the first year but was reminded of it several years later when I moved to Nottingham and applied for a car loan from the council. Apparently, I was offered the loan, in writing, on exceedingly favourable terms, as I was not classified as an essential car user. I signed the document and returned it but was then called for an interview with the deputy chief executive, who told me a mistake had been made and I would have to sign another document offering me the loan on less favourable terms. When I refused, he mentioned the 'Sociology of Deviancy' course I had included on my CV, and he asked me whether my refusal was part of the deviancy I had learnt when undertaking it! He noted that I could have a good career in Nottinghamshire but my lack of cooperation on this matter might hinder this happening. I held firm and the council decided to grant me the loan on the terms laid out in the document I had already signed!

After more than two years as a senior social worker, all the social workers in our borough were called out on official strike by our trade union, NALGO, as part of a national dispute regarding pay and conditions for local government workers. I was to be on strike for more than six months. Although we received full pay from NALGO, it was a difficult time, with picketing taking place during the early part of what was later to be called the Winter of Discontent. I was a member of the local Strike Committee and was involved in picketing five days a week and helped with the collation and distribution of a local newsletter.

My involvement in the strike only came to an end in January 1979 when I got a new job as a senior social worker in Nottingham. The decision to leave, in the circumstances, was a difficult one, but I had been considering leaving London for some time. A personal matter described in the next chapter was very much involved in my decision.

# 7.
# THE YOUNG LOVER

I met Lorna the first day I started work as an assistant childcare officer in London. She was given the task of looking after me a bit and I accompanied her on some visits. She was pretty, blonde and slim, with an engaging personality, and she had got married six months before. I worked with her regularly over the next two years and was soon to fall in love with her.

There was no love at first sight. I simply got close to Lorna by talking to her and working with her most days in what was a stressful environment. I learnt a lot from her, as I did from other members of the social work team, but in Lorna's case, my affection, admiration and respect grew. We also laughed a lot in each other's company. While all the team worked well together and sometimes socialised, I realised gradually that I was very fond of her. I remember work trips we undertook together to visit children in care, and one concessionary day we spent together with other members of the team visiting Cambridge. However, one day, after about 18 months, it suddenly dawned on me that I was madly and hopelessly in love with her. I had never been in love in this same way before with my emotions seemingly out of control. I was both shocked and somewhat bewildered, especially given my family background, where most emotions were kept under lock and key. It was as though all my emotional experience had suddenly crept up on me and all my emotional defences had been breached.

Soon after, Lorna let me know that her application to undertake social work training at Bedford College in London had been successful and that she would be leaving work on a one-year secondment two months later. I did not know how to respond. I had not shared my feelings with her, but the day she was leaving, she asked me over to her house, which was near the office, for a cup of tea. She made the tea, sat me down and then told me that she loved me. I was very shocked but also in ecstasy. I had come to believe that she cared about me as a friend, but with her leaving, I had resigned myself to our existing and developing relationship coming to an end or at least being put on hold for the length of the secondment. The next day I was going on holiday with Cathy to the Lake District, so I had over a week to think about everything, although I had already agreed to meet Lorna when I got back to London. I was both happy that Lorna loved me but also guilty and distressed about Cathy because I knew that I would have to break up with her. I told Cathy, while we were away, that I had fallen in love with someone else. She had already met Lorna on various social occasions involving my work. As Cathy and I had been living together for several years, it was a very difficult time, as she fought for me to stay with her. The holiday was of course ruined. I felt very guilty, but I was sure that we would have to separate. I told her that we had to part.

When we got back to London, I arranged to see Lorna straight away in Lewisham, where she was doing a social work placement as part of her course. It was a cold September night and we sat on a bench for some considerable time next to the pond in Blackheath. I was so happy that she'd said she loved me. We kissed for the first time and arranged to meet again soon after. Cathy had by now left our flat in North London, so Lorna arranged to see me there. As it happened, I got the flu in the meantime and was quite ill for a few days – but she still came and sat on my bed. We talked and talked, but nothing else happened. It was a week or two later that our love affair really began.

For the next 8 months we were lovers. As a poet once said, it was 'a brief, dreamy, kind delight', and I was both extremely happy when I saw her and very sad and distressed when we were parted. The strength of my feelings shocked me, especially as already stated I was not used to expressing emotions when I was growing up. I really felt emotionally close to someone for the first time in my life. It was precious but somewhat bewildering. I soon felt emotionally dependent on her. The intensity of the sex was overwhelming. Just touching her sent shivers through my body. The feelings she had for me were also intense and extreme. I knew how much she wanted me. She told me how much she loved me. I recall one day her visiting me and then leaving under my pillow a record, which was the Stevie Wonder song 'You Are the Sunshine of My Life'. It certainly did not feel like just an affair. As well as meeting at my flat and her house, we sometimes met in parks, including Highgate and Regent's Park. I recall our meeting in Highgate in the early spring when we had an afternoon tea together. I would also meet her when she went late-night shopping on a Thursday to Selfridges and other stores in Central London. We never had a meal out together or went to the cinema or theatre.

We talked about everything and often about her leaving her husband. She told me that she had met her husband after her previous boyfriend had ended their relationship. They had got together when she was very much on the rebound and that he had provided her with security. She seemed committed to me, despite my left-wing politics and my lack of financial resources. Then, just after the Easter holiday, I received a letter from her, in which she said that she had told her husband about our relationship and if I tried to see her again, she would kill herself. I remember going to work on the day I got the letter but being in a state of shock and emotional turmoil. I could not work. I left and took the underground into Central London. I went to the cinema and saw the film *Last Tango in Paris*. I felt terrible and was in despair. I did not know what to do. Of course, I wanted to see her, but probably, wrongly, I waited two weeks before I contacted her.

When I did see her, she expressed anger, stating that if I'd really loved her, why had I not contacted her immediately despite the threat in her letter to do herself harm. We talked a lot about what had happened and soon the affair had restarted. Despite the pain and the emotional rollercoaster, I could not stop myself and felt I had to continue seeing her. Once, she cancelled coming to see me by leaving a message with my neighbour, and I was again in total despair. On two occasions, she left her husband, the longest period being two weeks, but then she went back to him. When she did so, I was totally dejected and felt I was a failure for not being able to convince her how much I loved her and to be able to provide her with the emotional security and probably the lifestyle she needed. She did not seem able to face the many changes in her life that leaving him would involve. Just before she went back the second time, we had a big party at work and I will always remember dancing with her to Buddy Holly's 'True Love Ways'. I also went with Lorna to see her husband, to plead with him to let her come to me, but he just wanted her to stay. We almost had a fight. I realised how difficult it was for him, but I could not stop myself from seeing her. I was out of control and I thought of killing myself. I also imagined doing her harm or throwing a brick through the front window of their house.

I knew that she loved me and wanted me, but she needed her husband as well. I believe she felt very vulnerable and he seemed to offer her the emotional and financial security that, for many reasons, it seemed I could not. As well as him providing her with some emotional stability, they had already bought their first house. Her husband was an economist working in the City of London, and he was from a prosperous middle-class background. By contrast, I was then an unqualified social worker with left-wing politics and no money in the bank, living in a small, rented flat with a shared bathroom that was also used by other tenants. Undoubtedly, I should not have been surprised at the outcome. The affair continued, though, on and off for several more years. I hated the way she seemed to be able to compartmentalise everything in a way I was unable to do. We had undoubtedly different types of personality. My feelings for Lorna were still intense and I could not break it off completely.

I did try to meet other women, but it was impossible. I also seemed to choose the wrong women to date. I very selfishly started seeing one woman called Mandy and the relationship continued for many months. She was bright and outgoing and had undertaken a mathematics degree at King's College, but she was somewhat neurotic and unstable as well. Additionally, she had some ongoing kidney problems. She also told me that all her sisters in the family had experienced mental health problems that had required professional help. She was extrovert and, in many ways, a very capable person who lived a very full, adventurous life. For our first date, she cycled to my flat in Crouch End from the east of London where she lived. Later, while we were seeing each other, she suddenly decided to take a trip from London to the Isle of Skye and hitched there and back! She had also previously dated a photographer whose nude photographs of her had been printed in a popular girly magazine. Unsurprisingly, I thought of her as the 'Ruby Tuesday' of the Rolling Stones song. I was fond of her but also disliked her some of the time. On one occasion, she took a drug overdose. Finally, after we had been to a party together in North London and she was feeling ill with her kidney problem, we had a row, and she took a second drug overdose after I left her flat. She had wanted me to cook her a meal, but I had left with the intention of doing some studying for the social work course I was undertaking at LSE. I was in the middle of writing an essay at the time and was up against the deadline for submission. She did not recover from the overdose this time and was found dead the following day. The coroner's verdict was misadventure, but I felt very guilty and I think correctly blamed myself. I reached the conclusion that I seemed incapable of entering any lasting healthy and positive relationship with a woman. Unsurprisingly, though, it was Lorna who comforted me during these difficult weeks and months and we were soon spending some time together again.

In the next few years, there were long periods when I did not meet Lorna at all. Our relationship was on and then off during this time. When it was off, I would sometimes see her at work but was often unable to talk to her. I remember passing her when she was chatting to another social worker. Such occasions were some of the most painful in my life. She later decided to work in Central London and she became a senior social worker there. I would sometimes still meet her after work outside Great Portland station and we would go for a drink together. We once spent time in a friend's flat nearby.

Lorna and I were to eventually part in January 1979, when I finished working in London and moved to Nottingham. She came to see me in my flat in North London for what appeared to be our final meeting and we said our goodbyes, but not before getting into bed. It seemed, in the words of Graham Greene, in a novel that we both loved, to be *The End of the Affair*. It was so hard for me to accept, although I had been the instigator of the move away from her. It had been, on and off, a seven-year affair. We did exchange regular phone calls to and from Nottingham during the next 12 months, which I found to be of some comfort. However, I could not phone anymore when Lorna told me she was pregnant.

# 8.
# THE FOOTBALL SUPPORTER

I had always supported Nottingham Forest, since as a child, I had lived in Nottingham at a time when Forest won the FA Cup 2–1 in 1959 against Luton Town. I watched them on television that day in black and white as they went two goals ahead before Roy Dwight broke his leg in the first half and they had to play the rest of the match with only ten men, as no substitutes were allowed at that time. They held on to win, although Luton Town scored one goal later in the match. It was very tense waiting for the final whistle and it was a great victory against 'The Hatters'.

My first live match had been a few years earlier when we lived in Newcastle, as I mentioned above. At that time, I would have been less than five years old and I recall standing on a box so I could see the game and the away team being booed as they came on the pitch. Once we moved to Nottingham, I then attended Forest home matches quite often with my father. They always played the Robin Hood theme tune as the team ran on to the pitch. Forest was then described as a yoyo team, spending periods both in the First and Second Divisions. They had been only successful in the top division during my late teenage years, by which time, I was living in southern England.

Anyway, when I was only twelve, we moved some miles away from Nottingham to near Loughborough and my father decided to support Leicester City, as the stadium was closer. It was never the same for me as watching Nottingham Forest. During that period, and in the following years, I took an interest and supported Forest from a distance, although I did not attend matches.

Later, when I was sixteen, we moved away from the Midlands and it would have been more difficult for me to get to the City Ground. It was, in fact, not until my late twenties that I joined the Nottingham Forest Supporters Club (London and Southern Counties Branch) and began attending both home and away matches regularly.

My greater interest partly arose because of the new manager Brian Clough and partly, I think, out of escapism as my relationship with Lorna became more difficult and spasmodic. Clough, after some early barren years, was to bring unprecedented success to what was a relatively small provincial club. In fact, when he became the manager of Forest, they were in the lower part of the Second Division and the club had even spent a year in the Third Division sometime before. The rebuilding programme took several years. However, along with Peter Taylor, his assistant manager, Clough was soon to steer Forest back to the First Division, although they only just achieved promotion in the 1976–77 season. In their first year back there (1977–78), he led them on to win the First Division Championship by toppling Liverpool, who, in that period, had seemed unbeatable to many people. It was a remarkable achievement that has never been matched in the history of contemporary football, even considering subsequent victories, especially in Europe, which are described below.

While still living in London, I attended many away games in that championship-winning year, as well as almost all the home games, for which I had a season ticket. Most notable was a 4–0 away win against Manchester United at Old Trafford as well as home wins against Arsenal and Liverpool. Forest only lost three away games in the whole of the season and no matches at home. During the twelve-month period,

November 1977 to November 1978, they were unbeaten in the league.

I remember travelling up in a coach to Old Trafford to watch the United match with both Forest and Manchester United supporters. On our way back, after their heavy defeat, we had to be quite careful not to further upset United supporters, who were already very unhappy. I recall that when a rather large somewhat intimidating United supporter approached me, I was worried about what was going to happen, but he had only come over to me to congratulate Forest on their performance!

Forest was not a team of stars, but Kenny Burns was exceptional as a centre back, having been transformed by Clough from a centre forward at Birmingham City. The Scottish winger John Robertson also terrified the opposing defences, and Viv Anderson developed as a talented right back who was soon to be the first black player to play for England. Clough had also bought Peter Shilton, the England international goalkeeper. In the two strikers, Peter Withe and Tony Woodcock, the team had a formidable attacking pairing. Other notable players included Larry Lloyd and Archie Gemmill. Above all, Clough and Taylor had developed a strong and effective team that played exciting, attractive football.

Beyond all expectations, the success was to continue for the following two years with Forest winning the European Cup in both 1979 and then in 1980. In the 1979 final, they beat Malmo of Sweden in the Olympic Stadium in Munich, after defeating the formidable Cologne by means of an away victory in the semi-final. I made the enjoyable trip to Cologne and we had a good night out in the city afterwards, although I remember being spat at by a disappointed Cologne supporter as we left the game. A large group of the London Forest Supporters Club then travelled by coach to Munich for the Malmo game. On the way there, we passed a Malmo coach, on which all their supporters bared their bottoms as we overtook them. It was certainly an interesting but futile gesture! Again, we had a good time after the match in the Munich bars that night.

In the 1980 final, Forest beat Hamburg 1–0 in the Bernabeu Stadium in Madrid after overcoming Dynamo Berlin of East Germany in an earlier round. By this time, I had moved to Nottingham and a group of us from work drove to Madrid for the final in an old, somewhat battered Volvo. My most important memory of the trip is what happened after the game when Brian Clough and Peter Taylor walked around the edge of the pitch holding the European Cup aloft. I was no more than a few yards away from them. I also attended the quarter final Dynamo Berlin match, which involved having to travel through Checkpoint Charlie in Berlin on an exceptionally cold night to see Trevor Francis, the first one-million-pound footballer, score vital goals for Forest. Prior to the match, the small band of Forest supporters was given a guided tour of East Berlin that included a statue of Karl Marx and a museum with a replica of the Hanging Gardens of Babylon. I was worried, when we visited this replica, that some of the Forest supporters might use their spray cans and inflict some serious damage. Fortunately, the tour went off without any serious incidents, except some booing when we passed the Karl Marx statue! In the stadium, during the match, there seemed to be many people wearing long black leather coats. I presume a lot of them were the Stasi secret police. We were a little worried on the way back through Checkpoint Charlie, with Forest having been successful, as we had signalled to the German border guards earlier in the day that Forest would win. Fortunately, there were no problems, although, as before, mirrors were placed under the coach to check that no one was hiding there to escape to the West.

These Forest victories and others, including League Cup success and a runners-up position in the First Division in season 1978–79, were magnificent achievements beyond anything that had seemed possible. Such successes in these three years have only been partially matched by the achievement of Leicester City (a similar size club) who won the Premiership in 2016, which was certainly a feat particularly impressive, given the much greater commercialisation of football in recent years.

Based on Forest's achievements, and considering his earlier success with Derby County, it seems to me that Brian Clough must have a case for being considered the greatest of all UK football managers. Clough's later descent into alcoholism and much poorer managerial performances should not detract from these amazing achievements. As a fan, I can only be thankful that I was there at the time.

Forest did continue, however, with some success during the 1980s. I recall one memorable evening in Nottingham when we played Glasgow Celtic. The Glasgow hordes invaded Nottingham the day before the event and there was, as you might expect, a great deal of drinking. In a pub before the game, I spent time chatting to the Celtic fans, who were engaged in double-fisted drinking – a pint of beer in one hand and a large dram of whisky in the other. They suggested

I attend the return match in Glasgow. I very much wanted to go there but work commitments would have made it difficult for me to attend. Such a pity as it would have been my only chance to watch Forest play in Glasgow. After a miserable 0–0 draw in Nottingham, our team went on to a convincing victory at the Celtic ground. I remember also having an interesting time visiting Brussels and watching Forest play Anderlecht. As well as recalling the match, I remember drinking a great deal of alcohol. The match became infamous because it later came to light that the referee had been bribed to throw the match in favour of Anderlecht. There were several controversial refereeing decisions, and Forest lost the game!

However, there was another side to football during this period that should be mentioned: hooliganism. Inevitably, I witnessed it, especially when I attended away matches, and on several occasions, I was lucky to get home unharmed. Among other incidents, I recall being surrounded by fighting on the terraces, most notably at Chelsea's Stamford Bridge ground, being protected by the police in one small corner of a stand that had been taken over by Millwall hooligans, and being followed across Manchester and threatened by so-called Manchester United supporters. The first incident at Stamford Bridge occurred when Chelsea's hooligans infiltrated the away supporters' end. Although the police were stopping possible suspects and asking them which part of Nottingham they lived in, these hooligans seemingly had no problem accessing the Forest fans' enclosure, despite their London accents. During the first half, there was a rumble behind me and boots were flying all over the place before the police intervened. Secondly, at Millwall, the small band of Forest supporters had, unwisely, at half-time, chanted at the Millwall crowd at the far end of the ground, 'If you want us, come and get us.' Unsurprisingly, as at that time there were no barriers stopping the hooligans from making their way from one end of the ground to the other, you could then track their movement towards us. Bearing in mind the reputation of some Millwall supporters, it was not a pleasant experience. We certainly needed police protection for the rest of the match! Thirdly, regarding the incident in Manchester, a group of us were returning from a League Cup game in Bury on our way back to London when, during our walk between the two railway stations, we were approached by a group of young men who had clearly planned to wait for Forest supporters crossing the city. One of this group came up to us and asked the time. In asking the question, we knew he was wanting to check our accents. He then went back to their group, who were clearly then involved in some heated discussion. Someone then shouted that we were Forest and 'would never make the train to Nottingham'. I think we were only saved by the fact that we were already not far from the railway station. We decided to make a run for it. The hooligan group did come into the station but were then confused that we were getting on the London train rather than the Nottingham one.

Additionally, on one never-to-be-forgotten occasion when returning to London from Nottingham by train, after Forest had played Chelsea, a large group of Chelsea supporters got on the train at Leicester with Indian takeaways and then proceeded to wreck carriages, break into the bar, which was closed, and steal all the alcohol, and also regularly pull the emergency cord and bring the train to a halt. I was asked by one Chelsea fan which team I supported and when I foolishly told him Forest, unsurprisingly, he swore at me. I could have reasonably expected worse to follow, but by the time we got to Wellingborough, the police arrived and we had a police escort, with the train stopping at every station all the way back to St Pancras. The police escort kept changing as well so that when we got towards London, we were met by new police with dogs, who swaggered on to the train and said, 'You are nearly home. This is the Met, boys!'

Finally, I want to mention one further bizarre incident that took place near Derby railway station when I went to see Forest play there. There was, of course, a fierce rivalry between Derby County and Forest given the proximity of the two cities, and because Brian Clough had been a successful manager of the Rams before he arrived in Nottingham. On this day, I decided to stop for a drink in a hotel bar near the station, along with other Forest supporters, after we got off the train from Nottingham. We were having a quiet drink when we realised that a wedding was taking place there. The bride in her wedding dress walked across the bar. Just as she left, glasses started flying in every direction, as a number of Derby County supporters had entered the bar (although, like the Forest supporters, they were not wearing their scarves). Although glasses were flying, nobody seemed to know for certain which fans were Forest and which were the Rams. In the chaos, I jumped over the bar and remained there until the fighting was over. Although with the glasses flying it was very frightening and dangerous, fortunately, at the end of the affray, nobody seemed to have been seriously injured. It was the last time I went for a drink near Derby railway station before a match there! I wonder to this day what the bride and groom made of it all.

Hooliganism was a serious problem during this time and it was certainly a deterrent, stopping many people and families attending matches. However, I think some of the ways hooligan groups operated were not entirely understood. In my experience, some of the leaders kept a low profile and did not appear to be leading. They were sometimes in the background, encouraging the others, and organising, but not at the front of the action when it took place – in other words, more like generals than front-line soldiers! I knew one of the hooligan leaders for a period at Nottingham Forest, but without inside knowledge, nobody would have believed he was involved in this way, as he appeared quiet and placid. I was later to read quite a lot of literature on the sociology of hooliganism while studying at Essex University, but the authors of these books and articles, in my opinion, did not always understand some of these dynamics.

# 9.
# LATER FRIENDSHIPS AND LIFE BACK IN NOTTINGHAM

Finally leaving Lorna and London in 1979 was a huge wrench. Although, as I stated earlier, we kept in touch by phone for more than a year, it seemed like the end and in some ways, my whole world had collapsed. At the same time, I had a new job as a senior social worker in inner-city Nottingham, with many work pressures and a heavy workload. Fortunately, this was also the period when a new friendship developed that was to sustain me for many years to come.

I met John on a recruitment and selection training course provided by an external consultant who also did work with big corporations, including oil companies. I undertook the course within one or two weeks of arriving back in Nottingham. We all had to fill in a detailed questionnaire about our values, attitudes, and decision-making, and John had the distinction of getting the lowest score and being told by the consultant that he regarded him as unemployable. I scored in the average cohort. I thought John sounded interesting and we were soon chatting. He worked with young offenders and despite his score on the questionnaire, he was soon to become a team leader. He was outgoing, humorous and fun to be around, and had been brought up in a miners' welfare pub in a pit village in Derbyshire. A long-term friendship soon developed and we became regular drinking companions. Every Thursday night, the two of us, and other friends, would go to the Trip to Jerusalem pub in Nottingham, which was built into the castle rock. The pub claimed to be the oldest one in the city, dating from the Middle Ages (1189). Legend has it that some of the Crusaders had stopped there before their journey to Jerusalem and the Holy Land.

My friendship with John that started at that time has continued for more than 40 years to the present. In the

1980s, we were to have many holidays and adventures together, mainly in Spain and Greece where we visited John's friends who operated a night club on the Costa Brava and then a restaurant on the Greek island of Zante. I would occasionally be a volunteer on the door of the night club in Spain while John was a 'waiter' inside. Free sparkling wine described as 'champagne' was provided. John would later recount an incident when he had his bum pinched by a young woman who was with her parents. She had probably drunk a little too much of the free sparkling wine!

On another occasion, we had been out drinking all day with perhaps predictable results. John had left the night club we had visited on his own, only to be accosted by a group of Germans searching for a Brit who had beaten up one of their friends earlier. John was attacked and then dragged to a coach to be identified. He was thrown off the coach when they decided he had not been involved, but in his unfortunate inebriated state, and without some footwear, he was then attacked again by a Spanish gang who stopped their car and approached him with truncheons. He had to give up his leather jacket before they let him go. After we had returned to the flat where we were staying, he eventually turned up in a rather pitiful and miserable state. The following day we were in the hospital getting him repaired. He was badly bruised and battered. John's wife and another friend who was in plaster and recovering from a broken arm were also on the trip. We had an interesting time driving back to the UK and stopping at hotels in France for accommodation. The staff on reception looked at us very strangely when the two invalids turned up! More generally, on these holidays, visiting Spanish hospitals for one reason or another was a common occurrence. It always seemed to be John who experienced the problems. Somehow, we still really managed to enjoy these trips.

We also had a good time together on holiday on the island of Zante, Greece. We surprised our friends on one occasion by turning up from the UK at their pizza restaurant without notice. Unsurprisingly, John finished up working in the kitchen some of the time. It would be true to say that the quality of the food left something to be desired. However, we all had a good time there, fuelled by a considerable amount of alcohol.

With regard to work, when I first moved back to Nottingham, the County Council arranged accommodation for me in St Ann's, not far from the centre of Nottingham. After a period sharing a flat in Sherwood just north of Nottingham, I was then allocated a council flat in Lenton, where I stayed for several years. I then finally purchased a newly refurbished four-bedroom terraced house in Sherwood with a small garden in 1987. It had been very pleasantly refurbished and redecorated and I was pleased with it. Someone had tipped me off that it was about to be put on the market, and I was able to put in an offer very quickly. It was definitely good value for money. I was 38 years old. Within a few months, I had a housewarming party that was very well attended, although I did manage to fall out briefly with John over a woman we were both rather attracted to.

Regarding work, during this period, I was supervising a team of very experienced social workers, but I also carried a small caseload, which offered its own challenges. The area we covered was one part of inner-city Nottingham, including the Arboretum, Forest Fields and a part of Hysom Green. It was in the Hysom Green flats in 1981 that a serious riot took place as part of the wider national disruption during that year.

On one occasion, I had to prepare a custody report in a complex and difficult case, in which the parents were separated and the father was contesting custody of his daughter, who was about 8 years old. (The daughter was living with the mother at this time.) He was also refusing to accept the separation from his wife and therefore she had stayed for some time in a women's refuge. When she had moved again, however, he had discovered her address and on one occasion broken into her new house and hidden under her bed to frighten her and to discover if she had a new boyfriend. Under these circumstances, I had to supervise access visits for his daughter in his home. In this situation, both he and other members of his family made various attempts to provide reasons to avoid returning the daughter to his wife. More generally, it was also clear that he was trying to manipulate his daughter's emotions to encourage her not to go back to her mother. It was dreadful, with threats, obstruction, and an upset little girl who was a pawn in the ongoing conflict between the parents. Although there were some issues regarding the mother's behaviour that could affect the welfare of her daughter adversely, which had to be considered, I believed there was no reason to alter the current arrangement in which the mother had custody. The judge agreed with me and thanked me in court for my helpful and detailed report. The access of the father to his daughter was restricted.

I also had, occasionally, other types of problems during this period. For example, I was once contacted by one of the assistant directors (not my line manager) and asked about a particular case regarding a teenage girl who had gone missing and been reported to the police. The assistant director wanted me to immediately drive to Sheffield to find out if she had gone to stay with her father who lived there, but I refused. He was very angry and said he was instructing me, but I told him that as, he was not my line manager, he was not able to do so. Not surprisingly, my own assistant director was on the phone a few minutes later, also stating that I should go to Sheffield. I told him that, in my professional assessment and that of the social worker, it was unlikely that she would have gone there yet and anyway the Sheffield police would be able to check. He was also very unhappy with me but did not insist. Interestingly, the next time I met him, he told me that he liked people who stood up to him, but that if I did it again, I would be out of a job!! Regarding the same father, I remember on another separate occasion having to visit him again with an experienced social worker on Boxing Day, also about his daughter, who we understood on this occasion was with him. As he had a long and serious criminal record for violence, we approached him with some caution. After we knocked on the door, he opened a window and shouted out that he was 'going to put our fucking heads through a window'. He then opened the door and let us in. Within a few minutes, his attitude changed and he was friendly and cooperative. He even asked us if we would like any Christmas dinner! We politely declined. We were subsequently able to escort his teenage daughter back to her children's home.

During this period, our team always undertook student placements as well. On one occasion when we had two students placed with us as a team, we decided with the involvement of the students and other partners, to undertake some research by undertaking a detailed community profile of one part of our inner-city area.

We chose the Arboretum, which was the nearest part of our patch to the city centre. It was a mixed middle- and working-class area blighted by some street prostitution. The profile was to include both demographic information and a description of available community resources. An interesting report was produced, which highlighted the stability in terms of demographics of the local population and the available community resources, some of which had been somewhat hidden from us previously.

After nearly three years back in Nottingham as a senior social worker, I decided to apply for a further one-year university course in Social Services Planning at Essex University. The course was led by the famous Professor Peter Townsend, who had written many books about poverty, family life in the East End of London, and on other matters. I was given a year's unpaid leave by my employer and was awarded a Social Science Research Grant to undertake the course. I found it interesting and enjoyed the interaction with the staff group and many of the other students. It also gave me time for some wider studying in sociology, as well as social policy. I remember considering Max Weber's theory of bureaucracy as part of an examination of how the social work service operates within the setting of local government. I also did some other studying in the areas of the sociology of health, football hooliganism, and social problems such as child abuse. Additionally, there were some interesting discussions on aspects of sexual deviancy with Ken Plummer, one of the tutors who was a specialist in that area. As there were only lectures and seminars on two days a week, I was able to travel down to the campus in Colchester early in the morning from Nottingham, stay one night with one of the other students on the course, and return to Nottingham the following evening. I recall the beauty of Rutland Water, as I would regularly pass it on the trip down at dawn as the sun was just rising.

Peter Townsend was a somewhat charismatic character, whose seminars I enjoyed. He was incredibly busy, not only with his academic activities but also with his involvement in lobbying and action against poverty. He was also constantly engaged with the media. One day he would be being interviewed by Japanese television and the next day he would be flying to the American Midwest. I recall on one occasion asking Professor Townsend what kept him motivated in his research work and campaigning about poverty and inequality, given what appeared to be a lack of success in achieving much reduction in poverty or in reducing inequality. He said that it was a bit like getting on one of the circular rides at the fair. Once you were on, it was difficult to get off! He was an interesting and bright man, but I could not help thinking that his examination of the causes of poverty required much more structural analysis of how capitalism operated with the result of maintaining or increasing inequality.

Overall, I enjoyed most of my year studying in Essex. The people undertaking the course were also an interesting group of mature students with a wide range of backgrounds in social care. We were supposed to complete the course during the summer months by undertaking a dissertation on a subject of our choice. However, once back in a work environment, I became distracted and although carrying out much preparation on the subject of 'Social work decision-making in local authorities', I did not complete the assignment. Consequently, I was subsequently awarded a postgraduate diploma rather than a master's degree by the University.

When I returned to Nottingham, I was offered a new job with the Council, developing mental health and learning disability services. It was a major change for me and I was to undertake this work for the next seven years. During this period, I contributed to the restructuring of mental health services and the development of many new services for people with learning disabilities in partnership with the NHS and other local organisations. I learnt a lot about working with service users and their families. I was especially pleased with the work we undertook with adults with learning disabilities, and parents, in developing new community resources in Radford and Clifton, with the range of new initiatives carried out with Nottingham Mencap, and with the large number of new accommodation schemes commissioned with Mencap Homes Foundation. It was a time when additional community care funding was available for community services and we took full advantage of this opportunity.

Regarding my personal life, I started a new relationship with a woman called Julie, who was more than 10 years younger than me. For a time, we got on quite well, but I knew that she would never be able to replace Lorna in my affections. After a couple of years, we gradually drifted apart but remained friends.

On the downside, my alcohol consumption was high during this time and it was too much alcohol that contributed to a serious incident I was involved in with the police while driving in the early hours of an April morning in the mid-1980s. In the previous four years, I had already had a couple of other driving convictions. On this occasion, I had stayed late in the evening, drinking in a pub in central Nottingham with friends and had carried on into the early hours of the morning, as late-night sessions were common there. As I had intended only to stay for a short time in the pub that night, I had taken the car and therefore, when I finally did leave under the influence of a substantial amount of alcohol, I decided stupidly to drive home. I arrived at a roadblock set up by the police about one mile away from home and was stopped. I was then asked to take the breathalyser, which I refused to do. As a consequence, I was subsequently arrested and charged. I had certainly behaved badly and in the months following, before the court case, I became very depressed. For a short time, I considered committing suicide and on one occasion drove to a tall block of flats in Sheffield, took the lift to the top floor, which was open deck, and considered jumping off. I decided not to. I remember seeing John about this time. He had just separated from his wife, so we were both in a bad state, but we did attempt to support each other. I went to court and was banned from driving, and fined. I was in many respects relieved. For the record, of course I do consider drink driving to be a serious matter and very anti-social. I am strongly opposed to it despite the motoring offences I committed.

I also had an interesting holiday trip to Ireland during this period at the time of the Troubles in the north with the Provisional IRA (Irish Republican Army) campaign and Protestant terrorists. I had begun in Dublin but later drove to Northern Ireland. As well as then viewing some beautiful countryside in Enniskillen, I spent some time in Belfast. I recall entering a pub there in the city centre and attempting to pay with punts, the Irish currency at the time. The payment was refused and I was viewed very suspiciously. When I was leaving, somebody jumped in front of me and took my photograph. I realised of course afterwards that it was a Protestant pub! I also perhaps rather foolishly drove down the Falls Road, which was an IRA stronghold, in a car with English number plates. On reflection, it seemed an unnecessary risk to take.

# 10.
# RUNNING MARATHONS

John was into long-distance running and I soon took it up too and became one of the members of the 'Nottingham Ferrets', an informal running club, many of whose members undertook half marathons and full marathons. Initially, for a few weeks, I only ran short distances, as I was overweight, unfit and had taken no substantial physical exercise for many years. However, surprisingly, in a short time, I was running with other members a six-mile circuit from a leisure centre around the University of Nottingham. We would also meet in the countryside north of Nottingham every Sunday morning for a long run on a hilly circuit at Blidworth. Later, I would join other Ferrets and Nottingham Rowing Club members in a three-stage weekly exercise routine that included a three-mile run, then several four-hundred-metre circuits on the neighbouring athletic track, and finally intensive circuit training in the gym within the leisure centre. The first few times I did it I was exhausted at the end and wanted to be sick. It was certainly good training for Nottingham Rowing Club members and it did help me to become a lot fitter!

While still unfit though, after three months and starting from no exercise, I ran the Pony British marathon in Manchester on a hot summer's day with another friend. I did manage to complete it in under four hours and paid the price by collapsing at the end after enduring an uphill gradient for the last six miles called Plodder Lane and then finally having to run up a steep hill in the final mile. I was encased in tin foil for the following hour. I also damaged knee ligaments, and following this event, I was unable to run at all for three months. My limited training had certainly not been the best preparation!

Fortunately, I was to learn lessons, to some extent, from what happened, as I did considerably more training, including a lot more running, the following year before I ran the London marathon with one other friend. The week before, as the final preparation for the event, I ran the first 20 miles of the Birmingham marathon. I still suffered in London, especially in the last six miles of the 26-mile race. The distress was as much mental as physical, as your brain is telling you to stop running every step you take, and each of the last few miles felt like an eternity. However, I completed it on Westminster Bridge in a respectable time of 3 hours 19 minutes and was within the first 4,000 runners to finish, despite not crossing the starting line (owing to the many runners participating) until 5 minutes after the official start. It was the second year (1982) that the London marathon took place and the *Chariots of Fire* film music played all round the course as we ran. Naturally, I got considerable personal satisfaction from this achievement, although it took me several weeks to fully recover.

I had no desire to run full marathons anymore, but later I was to complete a couple of half marathons. I finished within the first hundred in the Nottingham half marathon one year in a time of 1 hour 24 minutes. As I was in my mid-thirties by this time, my performance earned me considerable respect. We had also encouraged a young man with learning disabilities to take part in this half marathon, as he had a reputation for always wanting to run everywhere. He did some training with us and was able to complete the course in a respectable time. I will always remember standing with him near the finishing line as he said repeatedly, 'I beat him', as other runners finished. It meant a lot to him.

With John, I was also to apply to enter, a couple of years later, the Barcelona marathon as part of a package holiday trip arranged by Saga, the specialist company for older people. In fact, when it came to the trip, neither of us was really fit enough to participate, which was just as well, as due to an administrative error on the part of Saga, we had not been entered. Fortunately, after we had expressed our psychological distress regarding the mistake, we did get a full refund for the cost of the trip! We also visited various drinking haunts in Barcelona full of verve and energy while claiming we were '*los maratonistas*' *who had* just completed the full marathon! Some of the local women were very impressed!

Finally regarding running, I remember one trip up to Cumbria when, rather than running myself, I went to support John, who was undertaking the Windermere Marathon, which involved a full circuit of Lake Windermere. It was a difficult course and I was to meet him at the 20-mile point with suitable refreshments. We had calculated the time he should be there, so I waited for him, and waited, and waited. As he was nearly 30 minutes late, I then decided I must have missed him and drove off towards the finish. When he finally arrived on the finish line, he was then to tell me that he had seen my car moving away just as he was arriving at the rendezvous point. To put it mildly, he was rather upset and angry about it. I just told him that he had been too slow! We had a good laugh about it later.

# 11.
# THE MANAGER

Although I had supervised and managed a team of social workers since the late 1970s, it was not until I took on the job of developing services for people with learning disabilities and mental health difficulties in Nottingham, as I mentioned above, that I assumed broader managerial responsibilities. With the new role, I became the manager not just for community teams but also for day and residential services. I was also responsible for commissioning services. In my view, the combination of the development role with operational line management responsibilities was very important in delivering substantial improvements to the service, some of which I have described in a previous section. It was also a time of opportunity with new policy initiatives on community care, legislation (especially the Mental Health Act 1983), and new pots of money (including ring-fenced community care funds and joint finance), which helped to facilitate the delivery of a range of innovative and exciting projects in partnership with the NHS and other local organisations. I was subsequently joined by two other newly appointed managers undertaking a similar role in central and northern Nottinghamshire.

In Nottingham, I had line management responsibility for about 200 staff and at the beginning I was on a steep learning curve regarding leadership and the various attributes of effective management. I also had to learn a lot about managing upwards, whether it was concerning my own line managers within the bureaucracy or in responding to elected councillors. In terms of outcomes achieved in Nottingham, I was viewed by most of my colleagues as being very successful, but I did from time to time certainly have my problems, not least the drink-driving conviction in 1985. Probably because of my successful development of services, senior managers were supportive of me at the time when this happened and I was not disciplined. Probably today, the approach taken would be rather different.

Our senior management was subsequently restructured while I was undertaking the development work in learning disabilities and mental health and, lo and behold, my new assistant director was the one I had refused to obey when that earlier incident occurred. As it happened, I then got on well with him. He subsequently stated, when making a speech to everybody at my well-attended leaving do in 1989 at County Hall, that at the time of the restructuring he had been warned that I was 'trouble' but that nothing could have been further from the truth. By then he was full of praise for my contribution.

Just eight years ago, with my friend John, we were invited to a reunion for staff who had worked in social services in the 1980s to celebrate the eightieth birthday of the man who had then been the deputy director. It was held at Trent Bridge Cricket Ground and many of the managers we had known at that time were present, including the ex-assistant director who had made that speech so many years ago. It was in some ways a strange experience seeing them all again, but we did have a pleasant evening. On the cricket scoreboard as part of the celebration, it read '80 not out'.

I left in 1989 to become a regional general manager in the southwest of the UK for a charity which was then The Spastics Society and now is called Scope. Getting one of the new regional manager posts was quite an achievement, as I understood that about one thousand people had applied and there were several rounds of interviews and other tests, including a handwriting analysis. In the final interview with members of the

107

governing body and the chief executive, I happened to mention that I was a football fan who supported Nottingham Forest. One of the interview panel then said that their chief executive was also a football supporter. I replied that was fine as long as he did not support Arsenal, and everybody laughed. He *was* an Arsenal supporter, but I still got the job!

I spent the next three and a half years managing social care, education and community services, and supporting local groups in the seven counties in the southwest of the UK. Working for a national charity was a substantially different experience from being employed by local government. However, Ken Young, the new chief executive, had previously been employed as director of social services for West Sussex, so we had quite a lot in common. He also brought a lot of baggage with him to the job, as he had been a very controversial somewhat marmite figure in Sussex and had eventually left there under a cloud. He was a straight-talking Glaswegian with a massive change agenda for the charity, which included a large-scale and systematic training programme. I was to get on with him very well. My managerial responsibilities included an education service in Plymouth and an outdoor education centre in east Cornwall. I had been given a brief to undertake a comprehensive review of the outdoor education centre, which was not self-sufficient and required a large annual subsidy from the Society to continue operating. The recommendations in my report involved a major restructuring of the management team as well as some changes to the service and the managing of income generation. My proposals were controversial. The head of the service was made redundant. While we offered quite a generous redundancy package, some lobbying took place for him to retain his job. It was unfortunate that redundancy notices were issued in December just before Christmas.

I was also involved early on in various negotiations with local directors of social services to develop new provision. Ken Young supported me in these initiatives and, after my first year, I was rewarded with a significant bonus. I would regularly attend the annual general meetings of local affiliated groups (separate charities) and spend much time with their representatives when we held regular regional committee fora. I especially enjoyed the contact with these local groups of volunteers who were based all over the south west from Bristol to Dorset to Penzance. I also particularly liked the opportunities to develop new services with local authorities and other partners.

The chief executive was, however, a very demanding person, whose managerial style at times was abrasive and challenging. He certainly took no prisoners and you were either on his side or against him. On one occasion, he invited the six regional general managers to The Spastics Society's national training centre near Henley and addressed them at length, stating that one of the six of us had betrayed him and he would reveal which one later in the day. He went on to say as well that if anyone breathed a word of what was said during the meeting, they would be sacked on the spot. Understandably, we were all terrified. Later, during a coffee break, he came over to me and said it was not me he was so angry with. In fact, he said I was doing a really good job!

Unfortunately, subsequent events meant that my fortunes went somewhat downhill from then on, as both Ken Young and the finance director were sacked on the same day by the chairman, allegedly because of a conflict of interest between their work for the charity and other activities they were undertaking. As the regional manager who appeared closest to Ken Young, I was immediately under suspicion and was questioned at length regarding my relationship with the ex-chief executive by the company secretary. Also soon afterwards, because Ken Young had developed a relationship with the head of personnel, which had resulted in them living together, all the personnel staff in the society were made redundant on the same day. A large number and a wide range of other staff lost their jobs as well in subsequent months, undoing the ex-chief executive's reforms following a series of farcical consultation meetings in Birmingham. The intention had been to make these various personnel redundant at these meetings, but after last-minute legal advice, decision on the redundancies were postponed until one month later. We still met all the staff groups in different hotels on Hagley Road but only for a general discussion about possible redundancies. In fact, they were all made redundant one month later. In the absence of any personnel staff, I was even asked to lead in the Society on human resource matters for a significant period afterwards! In my view, it was no way to manage an organisation.

Although I continued to work for The Spastics Society, which was soon to become Scope, for another two years the writing was already on the wall. I got on well with the other regional managers, but I became increasingly alienated from some of the directors and one or two members of the ruling council. I was also involved in a dispute over what support had been provided to one of the local volunteer groups.

I eventually resigned and decided to travel round the world. My managerial career would continue when I returned to the UK and got a job managing services for people with learning disabilities in Greenwich. I will say more about that later.

# 12.
# THE TRAVELLER
# ONCE MORE

My motives for leaving the UK in 1993 were mainly related to my continuing unhappiness at work, but difficulties with the job were not the only reason. I had been having an affair with a married woman named Andrea, based in the south west for the previous three years, and it seemed to be coming to an end. We had experienced some good times, including weekends together, but the closeness between us had definitely begun to evaporate. She was a vivacious attractive blonde who had in many respects initiated the relationship but had now been giving me various indications that she did not want it to continue, without saying anything explicit. I was also uncertain about what I wanted. Travelling around the world was a way of bringing the affair to an end or at least of being able to reflect upon what had been happening and the associated feelings from some distance away.

I travelled on my own and was away for three months, although on the morning of my outward-bound flight, I got stuck for almost one hour in the lift of my hotel as I was preparing to leave. Fortunately, an engineer got me out and I was still able to make the flight in time. I was to visit Thailand, Hong Kong, the Philippines, Australia, New Zealand and the west coast of the United States. It was a special trip and I enjoyed a lot of it, although I was a little lonely at times. I had never been before to Asia or Australasia, so everything was new and there was much to discover.

My first stop was in Bangkok, Thailand, and although I was soon to like the city, it was certainly a shock to the system, especially the traffic, which was overwhelming and described appropriately as 'gridlock' by the English language-speaking newspapers such as the *Bangkok Post*. At that time, there was no Skytrain and no Underground. You seemed to have to take your life in your hands just to cross the road. Besides the traffic, though, there was much of interest and a lot to excite the tourist, not least the beauty of many Thai women. I visited all the usual tourist sites, including the Golden Temple and some of the girly bars. I was reluctant to leave after a fortnight but got on the plane for my next stop in Hong Kong.

I stayed in Kowloon but took the boat across the harbour to Hong Kong Island. I also visited the New Territories. While I was uncomfortable with the strident commercialism and unfettered capitalism of what was still in 1993 a British Colony, I did like some of old Hong Kong on the main Island and in the New Territories. I was also much impressed by the amazing natural harbour. I thought about what the Colony must have been like decades before, especially with the bars and the nightlife, as well as the old temples, one of which I visited in the New Territories. I had daydreams about Susie Wong! However, as I indicated above I was unsettled by the commercial and competitive culture I experienced. Moreover, on the last night there, I had a curry that disagreed with me and developed what I self-diagnosed as food poisoning. I did manage to get on the plane for Manila, the Philippines, the following morning, but I felt ill all the way there. I was not disappointed to be leaving Hong Kong.

Manila was another shock, especially the poverty and deprivation, which could be viewed in many parts of the city. For example, at every set of traffic lights, young children would knock on the windows begging for money or trying to sell items of little value. The Philippines was the poorest country I had ever visited and my feelings about my stay there did not improve when I was warned by the staff in the rather run-down hotel I occupied that it was not safe to walk by the beach at night. They were right, as I heard gunfire on my first evening. Of course, there were still places of interest to visit as well as the multi-decorated jeeps all over the place to view. I visited a local Australian Bar with female dancers, but it bore no comparison to Thailand. However, the so-called Business District did offer a more pleasant atmosphere and it did have some more attractive bars and restaurants. It was in one of these bars that I got on well with a waitress, whom I invited to have some food and drinks with me later. We finished up in a karaoke bar on the top floor of one of the hotels, which had a panoramic view of the Manila skyline. I was only to spend time with her that one evening. But overall, I was far from impressed with Manila. However, I did manage to get out of the city for a short time and visited a lake and an old volcano. This rural scenery was much better than the environment in the city.

Unfortunately, while in Manila, I began to experience problems with my throat, which deteriorated to the extent that I almost lost my voice. I suspected that the painful and sore throat was caused by the unsatisfactory air conditioning in the hotel. Anyway, after a few days, I was back on the plane and heading for Sydney, Australia. By the time I arrived, I had lost my voice completely and was soon seeking medical treatment. The good news was that I recovered after a few days of treatment.

The largest city in Australia was everything that Manila was not. It had beautiful scenery and an amazing harbour and lots of exciting tourist sites, including The Rocks, the Opera House, and of course Sydney Harbour Bridge. I was also fascinated by the various seemingly affluent and large social clubs that, besides extensive bars, had various gambling activities on the premises. I was a little surprised to find there was no Foster's lager on sale given its prevalence in the UK, although there was plenty of Tooheys Red, Tooheys Blue and Castlemaine.

I also undertook a brief visit to a few of the sites in the Blue Mountains involving some lovely scenery. Later, I flew up the coast to tropical Queensland and the Great Barrier Reef, although I was quite disappointed with Cairns, which struck me as a rather uninteresting town. The Great Barrier Reef I visited on a flat-bottomed boat so that you could view the marine life underneath, was far more interesting. After two weeks, I was onwards to New Zealand.

I began my visit in Christchurch on the South Island, which the tourist guides tell you is the city most like many in England with its river, weeping willows and green scenery. In my view, they were right. (Of course, this pleasant perception has been altered in a major way by the recent earthquake). On the first night, I walked into the centre of town and heard Irish music and, as in most large cities in the world, I came across an Irish pub. It was a good night. I then hired a car and undertook a trip around South Island, travelling first across the Southern Alps. It was certainly spectacular and I would recommend the mountain scenery of this area to anyone. I also visited a glacier coming down to the sea and spent a very pleasant couple of nights in Queenstown surrounded by the mountains. In my experience, South Island was one of the most beautiful places I have ever visited, rivalling Switzerland and in a different way the English Lake District. Afterwards, I drove the car to Wellington and then, on the ferry, travelled across the straights to the North Island. As the mountains there have much more volcanic activity,

I was able to view a live volcano on my way up to Auckland. After a couple of nights in the city, I then took the trans-Pacific flight to Los Angeles and the final leg of my round-the-world adventure.

I used Los Angeles as a base but spent more time elsewhere while I was in California. I hired a car and drove up the west coast to San Francisco, which is said to be the most liberal city in the United States. I very much liked the place and would have been happy to stay longer than a few days. I also enjoyed the Pacific Highway drive with its wonderful scenery, which I travelled along on the way back. There followed a brief trip to San Diego, including a visit across the border to Mexico, and then a car drive inland to Las Vegas. The city was what I had expected – a long main strip of huge neon-lit hotels and casinos with fantasy facades set in the middle of the desert. I did not spend much time in the casinos but did manage to take the car on a one-day excursion across the high desert. The weather was pleasant, hot and sunny and some locals encouraged me to take the 'scenic route' back. I soon found myself driving up a large mountain. To my surprise, given the lovely weather until then, dark clouds appeared and it began to snow with some force and there were soon snowdrifts on the ground. I started to panic, as I was completely unprepared for this weather, and was worried that I would not be able to get to the top of the mountain. Also, I had no warm clothing at all. Fortunately, I made the peak and then could see the lights of Las Vegas below. I was very relieved to get back. I had certainly learnt a hard lesson that you should not take for granted any place that you do not really know. A week later, I was flying home to England from Los Angeles.

# 13.
# A NEW JOB AND
# LOVE RETURNS

It took me three months after returning to the UK to get a new job managing services for people with learning disabilities in Greenwich, south-east London. I started there in something of a crisis, as new proposals to change the day services and save money had resulted in many service users and their families being offered reduced provision. My advice to Greenwich councillors and senior managers, in the context of strong lobbying from Greenwich Mencap and many local families, was that they should accept that some mistakes had been made and that resources removed should be restored but then used rather differently in the future.

The proposals I prepared were accepted. After much hard work by me, and many other staff, in partnership with other agencies, users and carers, a new, more innovative day service was delivered. Radical plans for modernising other local services were also drawn up and over the next few years also implemented. Greenwich Learning Disability Services, which were already well developed in many respects, were then subsequently to get strong positive feedback from independent inspectors, win many national awards, and later be given national Beacon Status for these services. Greenwich Council was one of only four councils in England to get this award.

I was to spend 11 years employed by Greenwich Council and for most of the time I enjoyed working there. Initially, for a five-year period, I lived in Thamesmead, which was only two miles away from Woolwich where I was based. Then in 1999, I purchased a two-bedroom top-floor flat on a new development next to the River Thames between Woolwich and Charlton. At the time of purchase, the flats had not been built, so I had to use my imagination regarding the view I was likely to obtain through the windows. Fortunately, I imagined correctly and although the flat was on one side of the building, it provided me with a splendid view of the River Thames towards Woolwich Reach. While there were many positives about living in the flat, many of the properties had been bought on a buy-to-let basis. There were, therefore, many changes of tenants and I did experience some problems with noisy and, at times, unsociable neighbours.

Major initiatives that I managed while working for Greenwich Council included a large-scale European Social Fund Project to develop employment services for people with learning disabilities, involving many local partners and organisations in France, the Netherlands and Sweden. The project included visiting the other countries and learning about their services. In Greenwich, as a major part of the new initiative, we were able to develop extra training courses with the local college, a new specialist employment agency, and a new social enterprise charity that made written communication more accessible for people with learning disabilities. Our staff and some users and carers were also involved in undertaking various presentations. I came to realise that working with colleagues from other countries gives you a different perspective on their culture and other matters compared with what you learned as a tourist. The various partners worked very well with each other and in addition had a good time socially. Moreover, there were some special moments. For example, on the occasion when our Dutch colleagues arranged for a young woman with learning disabilities from our group to visit the grave of her uncle who as a parachutist had died in Arnhem during the Second World War. The UK aspects of the project were subsequently independently inspected by the

Government of London office. The inspectors later reported to me, as project leader, that they were so impressed to the extent that they stated it was the first project they had visited that did not require them to make any recommendations at all for improvement! I was of course well pleased, as were our partners.

We had a new director of social services several years after I began my work for Greenwich Council. He was dynamic and supportive and he trusted me to get on with my job with little interference. He also had good relationships with the councillors. It was a positive period when many service developments were achieved. Other heads of service and I, along with the director, formed the senior management team for the department. I was also involved in carrying out various wider corporate duties, and when the director became the president of the Association of Directors of Social Services (ADSS), I was one of two senior managers who regularly covered for him regarding his duties in Greenwich. Within another year or two, the director, who was undoubtedly ambitious, was to leave Greenwich and undertake national roles. For a significant period he was to be in charge of the Care Quality Commission with responsibilities for the regulation of both the NHS and adult social care.

Regarding my leisure and travelling during this period, I had, after my initial visit to Thailand in 1993, visited the country several more times. One trip included exploring Chiang Mai in the north. Additionally, on a trip to Penang in Malaysia with Phung, a Chinese friend who was a senior manager from work, I had also travelled overland to the border town of Hat Yai. These trips were pleasant, but nothing remarkable happened.

During this period, I also took other holidays abroad, including one to Budapest with John.

However, in 2001, my personal life was to change in a positive and dramatic way – in fact, in two very different ways.

First, I took another holiday in Thailand and to my surprise in a small restaurant bar in Bangkok met Parinya, the woman who two and a half years later would come to live in the UK and be my wife. As previously I'd had no intention of getting married, this was certainly unexpected and a major shock. However, it soon became inevitable in terms of the mutual feelings involved and was very much a delight.

Within a few days of meeting Parinya, I had persuaded her to take a trip to Chiang Mai in the north with me. We spent a few days there, told each other a lot about what had happened in our lives and soon became emotionally close. She cried a lot when she spoke about what she had experienced in her past. She managed in a few days to get through to me emotionally in a way nobody had since Lorna. She was bright, attractive, vivacious, thoughtful and caring, but also vulnerable. I wanted to protect her. Her English was still quite poor but sufficient for us to be able to understand each other using some non-verbal communication and signs as well. For that reason, Chiang Mai will always be a special place for the two of us. We made the usual tourist visits while we were there, including a taxi ride up the mountain to Doi Suthep, the Buddhist temple overlooking the city. I later returned to Bangkok for a few days and by then I knew I was fully committed to Parinya and that I would ask her to be my wife.

I better understood during this period that loving someone takes many different forms and no two loves can be the same. I soon felt very close emotionally to Parinya and we had a lovely sexual relationship, but inevitably I think the emotional intensity of the relationship with Lorna was not to be repeated in the same way. I believe looking back that if such intensity had reoccurred, it probably would have destroyed me. I suppose what two people bring to any relationship is unique, and as a close relationship develops, different qualities are brought to the fore. I was soon very much in love with Parinya, but being in love with her felt a lot different from the love I had experienced with Cathy and Lorna.

In fact, I was soon taking a trip with Parinya to Buriram, her home province, where in Tabak village, Chan Dum, near Prakhon Chai, I met many members of her family, including her father who was a rice farmer and who for a considerable period had also been head man of the village. He was a very interesting man who had been in the army when younger and had later when back in the village tried to protect the natural environment against further damage and destruction. Her mother had died when she was 19 years old. She had three older sisters and three younger brothers and had looked after her brothers when her mother had died. All her sisters continued to live in the village while two of her brothers were working in Bangkok, one in security for the Thai Air Force and the other as a policeman. I was to meet all her siblings within a few months. I was to like Pairote, the oldest brother, and Pu, his wife very much. Pairote was a policeman and his wife was a nurse.

The family house in the village was a wooden structure with a ladder to climb to the main living quarters. Various animals could be sheltered below. It was there that I spent my first night in the village.

The toilet was outside and during the night, after one or two beers, I needed to visit it. To my shock, when I got inside and put a torch on, I noticed a black scorpion on the wall. I was in no hurry to undertake any more night visits to the toilet after this experience! I only learnt later that it was the small brown one rather than the black scorpion that you had to worry about most, as its sting was much more poisonous.

I later realised that as a *farang* [foreigner], I had not immediately understood the significance of my visit. Family members had tied golden threads around my right wrist. Parinya, by bringing me to the village, was showing to people that I would be her future husband. The village was certainly a culture shock, but my commitment to Parinya remained constant. It was extremely difficult leaving her in Bangkok when I was due to fly back to England. I promised to return to Thailand within a few months.

Secondly, within two months of having met Parinya in Thailand and returning to the UK, an amazing event occurred while I was working in my office. Lorna, whom I had not seen for more than 20 years, walked down the corridor for a meeting with the director. Unsurprisingly, I thought I had seen her several times during those many years, but this time it was for real. She did not recognise me, but I immediately knew who she was. We were soon chatting about the last 20 years and what had happened. The meeting was very strange yet extremely special. All the old emotions that had been buried for so long resurfaced. All the love and affection on my part seemed to return as well as all the sadness and despair about losing her. It was also a huge shock. She was in good health and the passage of time had been good to her. She was working as an independent guardian *ad litem* for children involved with the family courts. She was very much the same person I had fallen in love with so many years ago.

We chatted a lot in the office that day and arranged to have lunch a few days later. She also came to see me at my flat. We did hug each other, but nothing more intimate was to happen. She told me that she was surprised that I was not married with children. I told her that after being in love with her I had not met anyone I had wanted to marry until just a couple of months ago in Thailand. Lorna had been working for a considerable time as an independent social worker and her husband, an economist, was continuing to work as well, although approaching retirement age. She also told me about her two grown-up sons. She explained what they were like (with very different personalities) and what they were doing. Additionally, for some reason, she told me about a recent affair now over – the first she had been involved in since our love affair so many years ago. I found it painful to learn about it. I said to her that I would always love her because of what had happened between us so long ago, but at the same time, to my great relief, I realised that I was no longer 'in love' with her. Finally, I told her about Parinya and stated again that I was intending to marry her. I had a strange feeling that somehow meeting Lorna again had finally freed me up emotionally so that I could marry my lovely Parinya. I was to stay in contact with Lorna for a while, mainly by phone calls but also via several meetings, but we both knew that there could be no return to the nature of our relationship before. Contact between us eventually ceased.

# 14.
# MARRIAGE AND
# THAI WAYS

I returned to Thailand in November, proposed marriage to Parinya, and we were soon engaged. I bought her a sapphire and diamond ring. Although I'd had no intention of getting married when I met her, I had realised shortly afterwards that I wanted this woman to be my life partner. She was pretty and very slim, with dark hair, brown eyes, and a lovely smile, on top of which she was bright, thoughtful, and sensitive. She was 35 years old. I began to learn a lot more about her background, including the various jobs she had undertaken, including rice farming, working as a builder, being employed in textiles and clothing, and in retail. She had even been trained as a soldier to defend her village in the early 1980s when the Thai Government was still concerned about possible subversion by the Khmer Rouge, who were still ensconced along the Thai Cambodian border.

She had been very much a tomboy as a teenager, which her mother had frowned upon. She had expected her to spend more time in the kitchen and learning other domestic skills such as the making of Thai silk. She had received an early proposal for marriage, but the boy's family had been unhappy about it because Parinya came from a poor family. Later, another boy had been interested, but she had turned him down because she was unsure about both him and his future prospects. Tragically, he was later to kill himself. Parinya had also always said to her friends that she would not be interested in dating a *farang*, so they were very surprised when the two of us got together!

As her English was still poor (although she already spoke Thai, Cambodian, Lao and Suay), we arranged English lessons for her at the Berlitz School in Bangkok and planned for our future. We also visited the village near Prakhon Chai again and I gave her father a letter asking for her hand in marriage. He approved but indicated that it was her decision. I also asked her to come to England for a holiday and she applied for a tourist visa. It was then that the nightmare with the British Embassy in Bangkok began, as after an interview her application for a tourist visa was refused, mainly on the grounds that it was thought that she would not return to Thailand at the end of her holiday stay. We were devastated. I could not believe that the woman I now loved would not be allowed to come to stay with me in England. The Embassy's approach appeared to be that any applicant was guilty until proven innocent. However, how you were to prove that you would return to Thailand after a holiday was unclear.

Over the next two years, I visited Parinya two or three times a year in Thailand, although this was difficult at times because of my work commitments. In 2002, we applied to the British Embassy after careful preparation for a fiancée visa. She was interviewed again by Embassy staff while I was back in the UK, and her application was once again turned down on similar grounds, as well as because of expressed concerns about her employment references and the financial information she had submitted. They also rejected her application on the basis that they did not believe, despite us submitting hundreds of emails and letters, that our relationship was genuine.

I subsequently made an appointment with the woman who was head of the section of the Embassy dealing with visa applications. She was very pleasant but warned me about the many Thai women who had many *farang* boyfriends and were only interested in taking money from them. Many individuals were opening multiple bank accounts to deposit the monies they had obtained. She also did not believe that a Thai father would transfer much of his land to one daughter, as had happened in Parinya's case. It had been done for ulterior motives. I explained that I was in a better position to judge the genuineness of my relationship with Parinya than she was and that the Embassy staff were wrong to turn down the application. I stated that we would appeal.

My visits to Thailand during this period were enjoyable but also painful when it was time to depart. I remember on one occasion early on arriving at Don Mueang airport in Bangkok (Suvarnabhumi was not yet open) and while still collecting my luggage from the conveyor belt finding that Parinya was standing next to me. Her youngest brother, Sanit, who worked at that time for Thai Air Force security had arranged for her to cross the security barrier to meet me. It was a shock but also a pleasant surprise. We had some lovely times and trips together, but on the other hand, I knew that when I was back in the UK, Parinya could feel quite lonely in her flat studying English, even though she had some good friends in Bangkok.

It was a difficult time for us when we were apart and on occasion, Parinya would cry on the phone when we spoke to each other. I tried to reassure her that we would win the appeal. In fact, it took almost a year to hold the appeal in London. We did not hire a lawyer and I represented our case before a recorder at the immigration tribunal. The Home Office was not even represented. I had printed out all the emails and letters between us, which resulted in me providing the tribunal with a large stack of paperwork. I received the decision some days later. The recorder found that the Home

Office was wrong in 'both fact and in law'. The Home Office decided not to appeal any further and Parinya was granted her fiancée visa. I had great pleasure in informing her.

During this period, on my visits to Thailand, I was beginning to learn from Parinya and others a lot about a new culture and country, which was substantially different from the UK and the European societies I was used to. My new learning curve was also complicated by the fact that Parinya's first language (and therefore culture) was Cambodian not Thai, so I was learning about two cultures rather than one. I also began to learn about the different lifestyles in the city and in the village. The main way to learn was from experience, but I also read some books that helped a little. One important lesson was about the importance of not losing 'face' and hiding feelings, which is much more important in many Asian cultures.

Another lesson was on the influence of various aspects of Buddhism, as most people in Thailand are Buddhists. In practical terms, this meant dressing appropriately when entering temples and removing footwear and not pointing your feet at people. The feet are regarded as being dirty and the least acceptable part of the body. A third lesson was about knowing everybody and cooperating in the Thai village. Although exploitation of poor people was taking place, especially by money lending with high rates of interest (and there were a few individuals who behaved like gangsters), there was also a lot of cooperative effort, especially at harvest time. The community spirit was also reflected in the celebration of Thai festivals. For example, during the Loy Krathong water festival in November, each village in the local area would build floats with flowers exhibited on vehicles, and then there was a competition between local villages as to which was the best float. I was to learn a lot more about Thai and Cambodian culture in subsequent years.

After making all the necessary travel and other arrangements, Parinya flew to Heathrow to live with me in England in August 2003. I met her at the airport and drove her back to Greenwich. She was not impressed with the smallness of my flat. I think she was expecting something more luxurious, as might have been seen in Western films. Another impression she had when we got back home was regarding the seeming lack of people who were outdoors compared with the many people out on the streets in Thailand. I had to explain that they were around but living indoors! There was certainly a cultural difference, no doubt partly explained by the large differences in climate. Unsurprisingly, it would take a while for Parinya to adjust to the new culture and the other changes she was experiencing.

An important new episode in both our lives was beginning. However, despite all the differences in culture, Parinya was soon adapting to various aspects of her new home and culture. She attended the local community college to improve her English, and in her first year, received a prize as the outstanding new student. Also, within two years, she was working as a cook at a local supermarket after we had previously arranged for her to study for and then pass her food hygiene examinations. She also soon had a circle of friends locally, who were both Thai and non-Thai. Regarding her family in Thailand, she maintained regular contact by phone and she was able as well for the first few years to visit them in Thailand twice a year. These trips were taken as our main holidays and provided, additionally, opportunities to explore most areas of Thailand. Places we visited included Ko Samui, Phuket and Krabi.

It was during one of these trips to Thailand at Christmas, 2004, that we fortunately missed the tragic tsunami that killed so many people. I remember being in a French restaurant in Bangkok just before Christmas Day with the people next to us discussing their trip the next day to Phuket. We discussed, ourselves, the possibility of taking a trip to Phuket but decided against it. It was on Boxing Day 2004 that the tragedy unfolded in Thailand and in other areas of Southeast Asia.

On another trip, I decided that I should visit the Death Railway near Kanchanaburi, which my father had worked on as a Japanese prisoner of war during the Second World War. Parinya and I therefore made the trip to Kanchanaburi near the beginning of the railway and after exploring the area, travelled on the railway to Hellfire Pass, which Australian and other prisoners and forced labourers had hewn out of the rock. It was not possible to go any further, as the railway track to Burma (now Myanmar) had been closed at the end of the war. When we travelled, it was an extremely hot day and you had to think of all the British and Australian prisoners and Asian labourers working in such conditions without water through the heat of the day. We later visited the local museum and the location of the famous bridge over the River Kwai. The original bridge built by the prisoners had been bombed and destroyed towards the end of the war. On the day we visited, a coach load of Japanese tourists was also there. There was a certain irony about this experience. We then spent time in the war graves cemetery. Those working on the railway were treated appallingly and of course many died (including the Japanese guards) from tropical diseases, including malaria. The Japanese samurai tradition meant that the prisoners of war who had surrendered in Singapore and elsewhere were treated with contempt. As I mentioned earlier, my father only just survived, as he was infected with malaria several times and on one occasion as I mentioned above was made to dig his own grave. I suppose I made the visit in homage to my father, but it was a disturbing experience. I felt it was a visit that I had to undertake, and Parinya was very supportive of me. I bought a book about the Death Railway at the museum and subsequently undertook some further research into what had happened. As I also stated before, my father never talked about his terrible experience in Thailand to me. I wish he had been able to meet Parinya.

Parinya had arrived in England in August 2003 on a fiancée passport, which was only valid for six months. We therefore arranged to marry in December 2003 with my mother and sister present. As my elderly mother lived in Cumbria, it was convenient for her that we decided to marry in her vicinity. We therefore chose Gretna Green Registry Office, which was just across the border in Scotland and only a few miles from my mother's home. Given the history of Gretna Green, as the place where young runaways got married, I certainly had never expected that I would be following them by tying the knot there! The registrar was friendly and the day went well. We had a pleasant meal and drinks in a local hotel. The following day we briefly visited the Northumberland coast and then York. Parinya was able to see her first snow in Yorkshire!

# 15.
# RETIREMENT,
# A NEW HOUSE,
# THEN ILLNESS

I was to finish working for Greenwich Council in March 2005 when there was a management restructuring and I was offered an early retirement deal. By this time, I was pleased to leave, partly because I was becoming more disillusioned with what was happening within my department in which we had a new director, and with other issues regarding the operation of the Council, and partly due to my new life with Parinya. I had several leaving events when I left. The first was with the local Mencap group, then with people with learning disabilities in a day centre, and finally with my colleagues and my boss. We finished up in a local pub and then had a Vietnamese meal. I was pleased that my ex-boss, who had gone on to greater things in social care, turned up in the pub. Some local councillors, including the leader of the council and the leading member on social care, also came along.

As well as getting used to life together in London and helping Parinya get to know the city and other parts of England, we made a new plan for having a base to spend some time in Thailand. We decided to demolish the old family wooden building in the village where Parinya and her siblings had been born and build a new family house with four bedrooms on the site. Parinya was to be the architect and work was to commence during the spring of 2005. She looked at lots of house designs on the internet and had soon decided what she wanted to do. She approached a builder who lived locally to her near Prakhon Chai but who mainly worked in Bangkok and asked him to lead the project. A lot of wood from the old family house was used in the new building, which allowed, in a positive way, some continuity to be achieved between the old and new houses. All the work was completed later in the year.

A blessing by monks was then arranged and a celebration party also took place for both the new house and our recent wedding. For the main part of the day, Parinya dressed in a traditional Thai costume, while I wore on top of my suit the appropriate Thai garlands. All Parinya's family and many other people attended, and we had two different bands playing music, including a rather unusual local police band composed entirely of ladyboys!

We also visited the Isle of Skye and northern France in 2005, but by the summer, I was experiencing health problems. It started with a pain on the right side of my abdomen, so within a week or two, I decided to go and see my GP. Initially, as the pain was not too intense, and intermittent, no immediate action was taken. However, I was soon at the doctor's again, and during that summer the pain got worse. I knew that something was wrong and my GP, after several consultations, did arrange for various blood tests. As I had been in Thailand recently, the possibility that I might have picked up some tropical disease was mentioned and therefore it was not a great surprise when the results came back indicating I had amoebic dysentery. Although I was somewhat surprised that I had none of the usual symptoms and of course wondered how I had picked up the disease, I was soon receiving medication for this illness, obviously hoping that I would then be cured. A couple of weeks earlier, my GP had also arranged for me to have an abdominal scan, but given the blood test results, he cancelled the referral, thinking that the problem causing the symptoms had already been identified.

Unfortunately, the pain in my abdomen continued and I began to doubt that the cause for it had been identified. I consulted my doctor again and he decided to refer me, again, to the hospital to see a consultant with the intention of arranging a scan. I finally had a meeting with a hospital specialist in early December and a non-urgent scan was planned for after Christmas. In the meantime, I went on a trip to Thailand with Parinya.

The abdominal pain was continuing and one day when we went to the cinema, I had to leave, as I was feeling so unwell. It was then that we decided we could not wait for the scan in the UK and I referred myself immediately to Bumrungrad International Hospital in Bangkok. After meeting a specialist consultant, I was referred for a colonoscopy the following day. I was given an anaesthetic to put me to sleep during the procedure, but Parinya watched it all. I awoke to be told that I had a tumour and the diagnosis was bowel cancer. Samples had been taken to confirm the type of tumour and its extent. I was also given photos of it and a video of the procedure that had taken place, which I still have. I met another consultant surgeon who offered me an immediate operation and mentioned concern about lesions on my liver that might be connected with the cancer. He explained that he could also operate on the liver if necessary!

Obviously, I was in a state of shock, as was Parinya, and we had to decide quickly what to do. While it was feasible to have the operation immediately in Bangkok, I was concerned about both the cost and the subsequent period of rehabilitation. I therefore phoned my GP in the UK and informed him of the diagnosis. He agreed to contact the hospital there and arrange for me to be seen as soon as I arrived back in the UK. We decided that on balance the best course of action was to return to England, and within one week of arriving back there, I was admitted for the operation, having shown the hospital doctors the medical report and photographs. I also had the DVD of the procedure, but no machine could be found at the hospital to play it!

We were both understandably distressed during this period, but at the same time, I was thinking rationally about everything that needed to be done to deal with this terrible turn of events. I was very worried both for myself and Parinya. While waiting for the operation, we had several visitors, including another Thai female friend, who would be supportive and helpful to Parinya during this whole period. My ex-boss from work (the current director of social services) also visited. It was a major operation and I felt that I had been hit by a bus afterwards, but the morphine helped. However, amazingly, I was only in the high staff support surgical ward for a few days. The tumour had been removed, but unfortunately it had gone through the bowel wall and possibly infected some lymph glands. I had what was called a Dukes 2, and I was soon meeting a consultant oncologist. His view was that I needed chemotherapy as soon as possible. He was keen to persuade me and suggested that if he had been faced with a similar diagnosis, he would have opted for it.

I asked for a short time to think about it and was soon examining the medical research on the specifics of my condition and the likely prognosis on the internet. The various research papers indicated that any chemotherapy treatment at best would improve my chances of the elimination of the cancer by one or two per cent, given the possible spread to nearby lymph glands. I then saw another oncologist a few days later and suggested to him that I did not want to put myself through an invasive course of chemotherapy with all the side effects if the odds for the cancer not returning would at best be only one or two per cent better than without such treatment. I was prepared to take what was a limited gamble in such circumstances. The second oncologist accepted my conclusion and did not try to persuade me to have the chemotherapy. I recovered gradually from the operation and felt almost fully better after three months. More than 19 years later, and after regular colonoscopies to monitor the situation, the cancer has not returned. I should add that my GP was also hugely relieved at my recovery, given that at one stage he had cancelled a CT scan. In the years after the operation, he certainly did everything he could to support me and meet any other medical needs I might have.

Being diagnosed with bowel cancer in Thailand, considering also the failure to diagnose it in the UK, was, unsurprisingly, as stated above, a huge emotional shock. In that period, I experienced many different feelings: not least fear and some depression. I wrote my last will and testament after the operation, and the experience was certainly to change, in some ways, my perspective on life and how precious it is. I believe that in these last 19 years, I have at least in some ways appreciated much more some of the important things in life – especially love, friendship and the beauty of nature. I had been allowed to continue with my life and for that I was undoubtedly grateful.

# 16.
# BEREAVEMENT

My father died in 1996 from a heart attack following two previous heart attacks, which had hospitalised him. I was working at the time when I was informed of what had happened and had to make my way immediately to my mother's home in Brampton, Cumbria. He had gone for a walk the day it occurred and collapsed. Local people had taken him into their house, but he was dead before the paramedics arrived. He was cremated a few days later. I remember going to see the body at the funeral directors and touching his hair and then saying goodbye.

As already stated, we had never been close, and during my teenage years, our relationship had been difficult. I know my father loved me, but like many of his generation, he found it impossible to communicate his feelings. For many years, I thought this inability was somehow connected with his terrible experience as a Japanese prisoner of war during the Second World War, but I later realised that our difficulties were much deeper and very much connected with his own family upbringing. While he tried to be a good father and was committed to my education and spent much leisure time with me and my sister, Elaine, I always felt closer emotionally to my mother. I did travel with him to many sporting events as I previously mentioned including Formula One races, football matches to watch Nottingham Forest and later, Leicester City, and some cricket matches, including Tests at Trent Bridge, but it did not bring us closer. I also remember playing cricket with him in Sherwood Forest and being with him when he was helping with the football coaching of my primary school team at Burton Joyce. However, again, I cannot recall such events with any strong feeling of happiness. It was just what we did. Reflecting on his death,

I regretted naturally that we had not been closer, but looking back I cannot see how our relationship could have been a lot more positive. Our difficulties were due to the nature of my father's personality but were also aggravated, of course, by my teenage rebellion. In retrospect, I wish that I had been more able to reach out to him. By contrast, I do remember as a small boy sitting on my maternal grandfather's knee next to their coal fire and feeling very loved and content.

My father and I also came to have different views about the world. My parents read the *Daily Express* and were politically conservative. Before the Second World War as I stated above, my father had supported Chamberlain and the appeasement policies. His thinking about the world continued in a conservative prism, and, given the deprivations of the war and the post-war period, both my parents (like many people of their generation) placed an emphasis quite understandably on security for the family and achieving over time a better standard of living. By contrast, I was part of a generation that would experience the Swinging Sixties when there was a much greater emphasis on individual freedom and expression. The music I liked was Bob Dylan and The Rolling Stones, and my politics as already stated were of the left, (although it was only at university and afterwards that my ideas developed in a more coherent way). My father wanted me to be a lawyer, but I was more interested in being a rebel. Of course, I was sad and distressed by my father's death, but most of all my feelings were about what might have been for both of us.

In different circumstances, it was 11 years later that my mother was to die of bladder cancer following a diagnosis that had taken place more than a year earlier.

There was no operation and no chemotherapy and for many months, no symptoms. I was certainly concerned that, no doubt at least partly because of her age, no treatment was provided. However, in the last few months, substantial pain relief was required and eventually, for what would be only a short time, she was admitted to the local cottage hospital. Prim (as I now called Parinya) and I had visited her the week before her death, but unfortunately we were not there when she died, although Elaine was present.

My mother deteriorated in the last few months mentally as well as physically, and in some ways, as she was in pain, controlled by drugs, it was a relief when she died. She was cremated in the same cemetery as my father. I recall the service, which was attended by some of the Taylor family, as well as my mother's local friends, and Elaine, Prim and me. I read William Wordsworth's poem, 'Daffodils', as part of the service. It was a poem that had been appreciated by both my parents.

I felt much more emotion about my mother's death than my father's passing. I had certainly been closer to my mother and I knew how much she had doted on me. I also felt for a time, as most children do, somewhat bereft by losing my second parent. It was as if an anchor had been removed. In some ways, I had probably resented what I saw as my mother's dependence and subservience to my father, but I knew how much she had cared. I was much closer to her than my sister, Elaine. Although Mum and I disagreed about many things, including my father and politics, it was a huge break to lose her. As she had also, in a few years of meeting, become close to Parinya, it was a difficult time for my wife as well. My mother had felt I was fortunate to have her as my wife.

During my mother's illness, I understandably had quite a lot of contact with my sister, discussing visits, my mother's medical condition, etc. However, it did not really result in us being any closer emotionally. In fact, during all the many years since she had become an adult, she had been emotionally distant from me and to some extent been similarly distant as well from our parents. While this did not stop us meeting up at Christmas when the family always got together, and on other special occasions, my mother used to worry about our somewhat unusual relationship a great deal. I suppose my mother's death seemed to lay bare my own relationship with Elaine. I have never understood why this estrangement took place as adults, although, as stated above, we had never been an emotionally close family, even during the years of our childhood.

For many years, my sister had been living in a bungalow in a village near Carlisle, having retired from her work as an agricultural accountant some time before. To the extent that we had knowledge of it, she seemed reasonably content with her solitary lifestyle, although we could not really be sure. She had never married or had children but had always been fond of horses and nature. We also knew, from what she had said, that she had been very fond of a man named David, many years ago in Devon.

I was proud of my sister in terms of what she had achieved. In her chartered accountancy exams many years ago she had obtained the top marks in the financial management paper and had been awarded a prize. Before that, she had attended university as a mature student after being employed for some years as a veterinary assistant and obtained a first-class honours degree from Reading University. She seemed to have had a successful career as an agricultural accountant.

After my mother's death, I had even more limited contact with Elaine, although on one occasion when we visited the Lake District, Parinya and I did have a meal together with her at her home. I have always sent her birthday and Christmas cards, but she has not usually initiated any contact. However, we did receive a card from her some years ago when we moved out of London.

I regret that we have not been able to overcome our lack of closeness or at least to understand better what has caused it. With my parents not being here anymore there seems even less chance now that we can get together and try to deal with what went wrong many years ago. However, it would still be good if we could mend what seems to have been broken many decades in the past.

One final note about the time my mother died. Parinya and I were supposed to be visiting Thailand with our friend John the same month she passed away, but for obvious reasons, we delayed our trip. John, however, decided to carry on rather than postpone or cancel. We therefore arranged for Da, an attractive female friend of ours, to meet him at Bangkok airport to escort him into the city. Remembering a tale he had told me a while ago about confronting a barking dog while on holiday in Spain when he barked back at it, and in the process losing his two front teeth as they sailed over the fence to be skilfully caught by the dog in its mouth, we decided that Da should carry a placard for his arrival saying: 'Fang Tours Bangkok'.

An account of the original event had, in fact, appeared in a local newspaper at the time and then had been syndicated to national newspapers under the headline, 'Dog in Spain swallows local councillor's front teeth'. (John had been a local parish councillor during this earlier period.) The joke was well received. By the time we arrived in Thailand later in the month, Da and John were already an item!

# 17.
# SAGA

After taking early retirement from my job with Greenwich Council in 2005, and after recovering from my major bowel operation, I continued to work part time in a self-employed capacity as a consultant in learning disability services to local authorities. Overall, I did some work for four London Boroughs as well as my local Mencap group. While some of the work was intensive at times, this flexible part-time operation very much suited me. The work itself was very variable and included assistance with a residential and supported accommodation reprovision programme, an evaluation of partnership arrangements for services between two boroughs, and a comprehensive review of day services elsewhere. Opportunities for such consultancy work became more limited, as local authority budgets were squeezed after the financial crisis of 2008/09 and from 2010 when the new coalition government's programme of austerity commenced. Anyway, by that stage I was becoming semi-detached from this area of specialist work, given the amount of time that had elapsed from my previous local authority employment. I concluded that it was by then time to fully retire. However, I did continue as a director for the management company for more than another seven years for the blocks of flats where Parinya and I lived, and during this period, I acted in the capacity of lead director working with the managing agent. A substantial amount of work was involved regarding various operational issues, financial monitoring, and in commissioning periodic internal and external painting. With other directors and the managing agent, I also had to help arrange and attend annual general meetings, ensuring that appropriate reports were available.

Once recovered from my serious illness in 2005–2006, regarding other aspects of my life with Parinya I was also active and quite busy. We had frequent holidays all over the UK and Western Europe as well as our annual trip to Thailand. During this period, we visited many parts of Thailand, including Ko Samui, Phuket and Krabi, again, in the south. We also had holidays in the Czech Republic, France, Germany, Switzerland, and Spain. These trips abroad became a lot easier when Parinya obtained UK citizenship in 2008, having undertaken and passed the exam on knowledge of the United Kingdom. She had previously only had the status of extended leave to remain and we had had to apply each time for Schengen visas for these holidays. We also developed especially a love of Italy and by 2019 had visited Tuscany, Venice, the Bay of Naples, Rome, the Italian Lakes, and Sicily. While for most of this time I was still driving abroad on these holidays, on the more most recent trips we decided on escorted tours as a more relaxing option. We used this arrangement to visit early on the Austrian lakes and mountains and then the Italian lakes and the Matterhorn. We enjoyed both trips a lot. Unlike some of my earlier holidays, when I would sometimes fall out with my travelling partner(s) on holidays, with Parinya we both usually had a good time!

We also had trips to many parts of the UK, including Devon and Cornwall, Scotland and North Wales. We have usually also had a trip to the Lake District each year, as we are especially fond of the area because of its scenic beauty. On one occasion on such a trip, we decided to drive over the Hardknott Pass, one of the most steep and difficult climbs in England. The road connects the eastern and western parts of the Lake District. It was a beautiful summer's day, but even so, the drive over the mountain in our Toyota Carina was hard. A four-wheel drive car would have been more suitable for the journey. We had a break at the top of the mountain at the old Roman fort. Our main companions were the Hardwick sheep, with a few other motorists also about. We did, however, later in the day get to Wastwater, outstanding for its amazing and rugged scenery. Our several visits to Scotland have included trips to Glencoe, the northwest Highlands, and the Isle of Skye. We have spent some time as well in Edinburgh, which we like very much.

More locally, I introduced Parinya, who was a Manchester United fan, to the pleasures of watching some of Nottingham Forest's away games. These included trips to Charlton and Crystal Palace and Gillingham. In addition, we went to White Hart Lane to watch Forest play Tottenham in a cup match. Perhaps the most notable visit, however, was to Millwall when we were not allowed entry, as they were banning all away fans, from some clubs, from attending because of potential hooliganism. I did explain that Parinya was from Thailand and not from Nottingham, but it cut no ice. There was some irony in banning us, given Millwall FC's own notorious record for hooliganism.

Parinya had also developed by this time a substantial friendship network of Thai and some non-Thai female friends. Many of the Thai women would often meet as a group and enjoy food together. Many of the friendships begun during this period have continued until the present, with contacts being maintained between both the women and their partners. These Thai female friends include Natalie, Sarah and Anna. Parinya developed one of her earliest friendships with Natalie, who was married to Don, an Englishman who worked for the local council. They had one daughter, and Natalie also had a daughter from her first marriage who was already an adult. Sadly, Don was later to be diagnosed with cancer and we tried to provide some support. He then suffered a severe heart attack that led to his long-term hospitalisation and during this time he was unconscious. We visited him in hospital until he died a few months later. Fortunately, Natalie has more recently been able to make a different life for herself with a new long-term boyfriend. Sarah has also been a long-term friend from Greenwich. She is married to Mark, an Englishman, and works as a dental assistant. Anna is a more recent friend, whose English husband, Lenny, died several years ago. She is now also making a new life for herself.

Additionally, a young Thai woman named Noy, who attended the same community college as Parinya for one year in Greenwich, became a good friend. She came from a similar background as Parinya in rural northeast Thailand and the two of them soon developed a close friendship. We got to know well both Noy and her English partner, Barrie, and we would often socialise together. Noy went on to attend the University in London, obtaining a first-class honours degree and then a master's qualification. In recent years, she has been the director of a bank in the City of London.

Unfortunately, a few years ago her relationship with Barrie came to an end, but more positively she was soon to have a new German boyfriend called Denis, who was also a banker. Before long they were planning their future together and were to marry in 2020. We attended the wedding and reception in London. At present, we remain in regular contact with Noy and her current partner, but we have also continued to have some contact with Barrie, who we also want to remain our friend. At the time of writing, Noy and Dennis have a lovely daughter, Clara, who is four years old, whom we have been seeing every year.

Contact and the exchange of photos with all these friends and many others is maintained mainly using social media including Messenger and Facebook. Social media and Skype are also used for communication with family and friends in Thailand.

From spending a New Year's Eve in a local pub, we also met Neil, a Chelsea football supporter, and another Thai woman who was his girlfriend. Neil lived in the block of flats next to our own and worked as an administrator for a financial company in London. His girlfriend at that time was on holiday in the UK. We subsequently got to know both well, although they were later to split up. Nevertheless, we have maintained some contact with Neil, who has followed Chelsea FC all over Europe and the United States. Unfortunately, not so long ago, he lost his job. He still visits Thailand and has sometimes asked Parinya for advice on Thai girlfriends!

While living in Greenwich, Parinya and I were not frequent visitors to Central London, but we did have a few trips a year. Highlights included watching *Swan Lake* being performed by a Russian company at the Coliseum, English National Opera, and a couple of classical concerts during the BBC Proms at the Royal Albert Hall. The highlight of the Prom concerts was undoubtedly Daniel Barenboim conducting an Elgar symphony followed by an impromptu short speech about education, enlightenment values and combatting radical populism. He finished off the evening by then conducting, as an addition to the programme, Elgar's *Pomp and Circumstance Marches*.

More generally, we have also increasingly taken an interest in some other classical music, especially Mozart, while not claiming to have any real knowledge or understanding of this genre. I had been attracted to Mozart's music since I was a student when I remember watching the film *Elvira Madigan*, which used his *Piano Concerto No. 21* as its main soundtrack. We would sometimes play his symphonies, operas, and some of his other music when at home or in the family house in the village in Thailand. I cannot explain why we are both so attracted to his music, but I do know that it seems to access our emotions in a special way. He may not have been personally an attractive character, but his music is undoubtedly sublime. When we were on holiday in Austria, we visited Mozart's childhood home in Salzburg.

Parinya also during this period took up a range of hobbies, including watercolour painting, jewellery making and photography. Other people, including me, were impressed with her paintings, which included many landscape depictions of nature. My favourite of her paintings is of Thai rice fields with two people harvesting the rice. Secondly, following a visit we made to Jersey when we saw a pearl necklace and other jewellery being made, Parinya started to make necklaces, bracelets and other items, usually obtaining the stones from second-hand shops and local markets. Photography became her third interest. We bought a good camera and several lenses and she was soon photographing much of nature, as well as the usual images of herself and her friends. Although these interests have waxed and waned over time, I am sure at least the painting and photography will continue to be important to her in her future life.

We undertook many day trips to the countryside to view and enjoy nature, especially in various parts of Kent but also elsewhere. We went to many places, but some of our favourite locations were the beautiful gardens at Sissinghurst in Sussex, which had been the home of the writer Vita Sackville-West and her diplomat husband, Harold Nicolson; the house and grounds at Chartwell, which had been the home of Winston Churchill; and Emmetts Garden with such a lovely variety of flowers, shrubs and trees. We also liked Whitstable, once a fishing village but now a town (but still with some fishing activities and vessels), and Dungeness on the coast, which appeared to us like a lunar landscape. The first three of these places were all National Trust properties and it was just as well that we had joint membership for this organisation! Through these trips and our holidays together, I came to appreciate the beauty of nature more and have increasingly felt closer to the natural world. Such feelings have me feeling more satisfied and happier.

I should mention one amusing incident that occurred on one of our visits to the National Trust property at Chartwell in Kent. The beautiful grounds were famous for having in the past a pair of black swans living on the lake, and the National Trust had maintained this tradition. Unfortunately, the resident male swan had a reputation for being aggressive and as the pair were trying to breed, he was in a rather sensitive mood when we walked towards the lake. Parinya went nearer to them than she probably should have done while I stayed further away. As I continued to walk some distance from them, I heard Parinya shout and to my surprise, the male swan, instead of attacking my wife who was nearer, was moving close behind me with his beak outstretched and his wings flapping. I had to run to get away from him! We learnt that I was not the only person he had tried to attack and the National Trust decided subsequently that the pair would have to live elsewhere. They were soon transferred to a nature reserve!

On our trips to Thailand, I would usually hire a car and we would drive around northeast Thailand, including Buriram and Surin. I did not drive, however, in Bangkok where I considered the traffic to be much too chaotic. My main concern driving was the risk of being stopped by the police, who I was advised would sometimes try to extract fines from *farang* tourists, whether or not you had committed any offence. Some of the driving was also dangerous, especially by children riding motorbikes, and the many adults who were often drink-driving. In other respects, I usually felt safe both in the countryside and in the cities. My only other negative experience occurred in a girly bar in Bangkok when I was inside it and Parinya was with her friend Da outside. After one or two beers, I suddenly felt very dizzy, although I was not drunk. Apparently, in my peculiar state, I then tried to leave the bar without paying. I was then brought back into the bar by a member of staff. Parinya witnessed what was going on, but did not realise there was anything wrong with me. Only after I was later helped home by Parinya and Da, did I realise that all my money was missing except for a 100-baht note (which was worth less than £2 at the time). Undoubtedly, money had been stolen from me, as I must have had at least the equivalent of a hundred pounds in my pocket that evening. I was in no doubt the following morning that a drug had been added to my beer, which resulted in my dizziness. I suspect that this happened when I went to the toilet and left my beer alone for a short time. Unsurprisingly, I never visited the same bar again.

When we were staying at the family house in the village near Prakhon Chai, Isaan, we would often visit local places of interests, often with Pairote, Parinya's brother, and his wife, and sometimes with their two sons and other members of the family. Pirote had been in the army before becoming a policeman and he sometimes took us on trips to small Cambodian temples on the border between Cambodia and Thailand, which in order to reach we had to go past army checkpoints. These border areas were still disputed between the two countries and there had been some fighting quite recently between the two armies. On one visit, we were able to meet both Thai and Cambodian soldiers and were able to see the bullet holes arising from the fighting. The area was surrounded by dense forest with signs indicating danger from land mines. It had been an area that had been occupied by the Khmer Rouge for many years after they lost control of the Cambodian Government following the intervention of the Vietnamese to end their murderous regime in 1979. When not fighting each other, the soldiers from the two countries still shared sleeping accommodation in a small hut! The small temple we viewed was exquisite. Parinya was some years later to take a car trip with her brother to Angkor Wat, the magnificent one thousand-year-old Cambodian temple complex near Siem Reap, which is not far away from this border area. I was also to visit Angkor Wat with her the following year. On other occasions, we also visited the magnificent Phanom Rung and the neighbouring Muang Tam temples in Isaan with Parinya's father and other members of the family. Phanom Rung, which is built on an extinct volcano, has its windows aligned with the rays of the sun in a similar way to Stonehenge. While located in Thailand, it overlooks lower lands in Cambodia. Pirote and Pu, his wife, also accompanied us one year to the annual elephant festival in Surin, which involves many of these animals enacting with their minders various historical war scenes as well as playing football and other games. We were impressed more with the historical pageant than with the training of the elephants to play games.

During all the time living in Greenwich but visiting Thailand, I became even closer emotionally to Parinya and our love and friendship continued to grow. We did consider for a time having children and I think would have fully embraced it if it had happened. However, it did not occur and the truth was that both of us were not that disappointed. It should be remembered that Parinya had already had to care for her younger brothers while still a teenager when her mother died and was now more than forty years old. Moreover, during this period, I was in my late fifties and early sixties. Considering these facts, living without children was certainly acceptable to us. I should add that Parinya has maintained close relationships with several of her nephews and nieces in Thailand, including Pirote and Pu's two sons, Python and Cheetah, and Amnouy's daughters, Sonwang and May. At one stage, Parinya started to teach Python and Cheetah some English via the internet.

In these years Parinya continued to work part time as a cook at a local supermarket, although for a three-month period from the end of 2015 to late February

2016 we had an extended holiday in Thailand, staying initially in Chiang Mai and then later in the family house in Prakhon Chai near the Cambodian border and then in Bangkok. Our friend John from Nottingham made the trip with us. During this time, Parinya was able to sort out various legal documents relating to her own and the family's ownership of land. She also purchased some additional land and supervised the building of what she called a 'greenhouse' in additional land we had purchased at the back of the house. We had some highs and lows on the trip, including various tensions which developed in the latter stages between John and me. Problems started in the village after John accepted an invitation to go and watch some cock fighting, which I had already turned down. I had no wish to take part in anything involving animal cruelty and I was angry with him for accepting the invitation. Other difficulties followed, especially when he got very friendly with Dum, my policeman brother-in-law next door, who often joined me to drink my alcohol and who I preferred to keep at a reasonable distance. John began supplying him with brandy. John became popular in the village and maybe I resented this popularity as well. Some tensions continued between us after we moved back to Bangkok. However, after 35 years of friendship, we were not going to let a few local difficulties get in the way of our relationship long term.

Our stay in the village had been interesting in other ways though. One of the daughters of the family living opposite had developed a reputation for meeting various *farang* men, becoming their girlfriend and then getting them to give her large amounts of money, with which she bought several houses. She worked as a tourist guide and had excellent English, which obviously made meeting these *farang* men a lot easier. Once each of them had transferred to her millions of bahts, they were then dumped. John and I, with Prim, spent an interesting evening with her and her family on New Year's Eve, which included us singing 'Auld Lang Syne'. Fortunately, we were not tempted by her charms to part with any cash!

In fact, during our extended stay, John had taken a special liking to Chiang Mai. I think this view was facilitated by a small music bar we discovered at the end of our trip that was frequented by many local *farangs*. As John likes to sing and listen to music, and as all contributions were welcomed, the place became, on a subsequent visit by him, very much a home from home, especially as the English proprietor and his Thai wife were very welcoming. As he started dating the Thai girl serving in the bar, this liking was very much confirmed. Sae-Lee [Night] subsequently became his long-term girlfriend and later his wife, and he purchased a bar/café with her. He now lives in Thailand full time. The first year's operation of the bar/café was successful with plenty of business, as Parinya and I witnessed when we visited Chiang Mai for a few days in November 2019. It was nice to meet Sae-Lee for the first time. We also met there again another friend called John from Nottingham, with whom I had gone to many Nottingham Forest matches when we both lived in London in the late 1970s. We had later spent a lot of time together when we were both living in Nottingham.

I also continued during this period to read extensively, especially regarding modern history. I recall reading several new books on the Spanish Civil War with the main focus being on the International Brigades, in particular the British and American battalions. I have always been fascinated by this period of history, given the missed opportunities that occurred in connection with defeating or at least containing Fascism at an early stage. I remain appalled by the policy of appeasement followed by the Western democracies during the 1930s. I continue to have a wider interest in modern European history and will no doubt always want to read new books on this subject for the rest of my life, although in recent years I have also been studying other aspects of history, such as the rise and fall of the British Empire, and Asian history.

# 18.
# A FINAL PLANNED MOVE

Back on the home front in England in 2016, we had negotiated a lease extension on our flat next to the River Thames between Woolwich and Charlton. When it was completed in autumn 2016, we acquired a new lease for a period of 170 years. This arrangement we anticipated at the time would in due course help Parinya with greater security for the future whether we remained in the flat or decided to move to pastures new, perhaps outside London. However, during the autumn of 2017, we gave more serious thought to a move away from London and the purchase of a house. After considering various areas, including the Yorkshire Dales and the Sussex coast, we began to give more serious attention to a possible move to Oxfordshire.

The decision to move was taken by the two of us bearing in mind several factors, including a belief that we had lived in London long enough, a recognition that we were living in a third-floor flat without a lift and I was getting older, and a realisation that at my age (then 69,) if I were to move, it needed to happen soon. We knew that we would miss our special river view and the friendships that we had developed locally, but on balance the positives from such a move seemed to outweigh the negatives, considering that we wanted to be at least near the countryside and to have a house with a garden. As it was only a few times a year that we ventured into Central London, moving some distance outside the M25 but within easy reach of London did not seem a problem to us.

We were therefore soon looking at a location along the M40 corridor in Oxfordshire because of the relatively easy access to Heathrow airport, given our regular trips to Thailand and other countries, as well as the relative proximity to London. For a time, we were keen on Bicester and indeed looked at quite a few houses for sale in that area. Unfortunately, or so it seemed when we were looking, we did not find any property that we could both agree was the home for us at a price we were prepared to pay. One house I was initially keen on had already been sold when I made a further enquiry, and one or two others that were identified and within our budget did not have the enthusiastic support of both of us. In fact, as it turned out, we were both subsequently pleased that we had not found anywhere in Bicester, when we decided to look a little further north to Banbury. We knew nothing much about the town at this stage, but of the first two properties we agreed to view, one of them turned out to be the house that we both concluded would be ideal for us. Although a three-bedroom semi-detached property and nothing special from the outside, the interior was attractive with a very pleasant conservatory, and there was a lovely garden. We made an immediate offer that was accepted and the move was soon becoming a reality, as we immediately put our flat up for sale within a couple of weeks, having already instructed a local solicitor.

Somewhat to our surprise, the move seemed to proceed smoothly. We sold the flat within a month, albeit for a reduced price but sufficient to ensure that we would require no mortgage. The only difficulty came later, as the previous owner of our new property had died in the autumn of the previous year and our house purchase was therefore subject to probate. In fact, we had been told by the estate agent that probate had been completed, but this turned out not to be the case. It was fortunate that there was not too long a delay, and with the help of our efficient solicitor, everything was completed. However, we did have to pay our existing freeholder, our managing agent and the Residents Association what seemed to be unduly large sums for their preparation of necessary reports and other documentation.

Preparation for the move in terms of boxing all our belongings proved to be a very large job even though we discarded many items we'd collected over the years. Like most people, we could not believe how much we would both be taking and how much needed to be discarded. We carefully selected a removal firm and they proved to be organised and efficient as well as reasonably priced. The move itself, with everything happening on the same day, was something of a logistical nightmare, but by just after 3pm that day in April 2018, we were already in our new home, surrounded by all our furniture and other belongings.

While it inevitably took some time for us to settle in and become familiar with our new surroundings, we are both very pleased with the move and are confident that it was the right decision for us. While the house was already well equipped and various furniture was left for us, Prim was soon at work sorting out what was a lovely if rather overgrown garden. We visited garden centres for plants and equipment on numerous occasions and the garden is now full of lovely flowers, especially bluebells, and tulips, as well as shrubs and small trees. We have a lovely maple tree, which has beautiful spring leaves and a small apple tree, which we purchased soon after arriving there. We can always also look forward to all the roses that bloom during the summer. In addition, we have many wild birds of different species enjoying the food we are providing. Our resident birds include robins, blue tits, great tits, long-tailed tits, blackbirds, sparrows, a wren, wood pigeons and starlings, while we have also been visited by goldcrests, greenfinches, a chaffinch and many others. Additionally, we have seen a sparrow hawk sitting on a roof near our garden. We purchased a barbecue soon after we moved and are making good use of it during the summers.

Regarding the surrounding area, we are on the edge of the Cotswolds and there are many picturesque ironstone villages with some churches dating from the medieval period within a few miles of Banbury itself. A little further away are some of the Cotswolds' highlights, including Bibury and Bourton-on-the-Water. Banbury is pleasant enough and has all the amenities, although the high street like many in the country is suffering somewhat from the competition with the supermarkets and the shopping centres. There are some empty shops. We do have though some historic and pleasant pubs, including one where Oliver Cromwell stayed during the Civil War. There is a wide range of restaurants, including Indian, Italian, Thai and Japanese. All the locals tell us we have moved to a quiet area compared with London and we are happy with what we have experienced.

It is also worth mentioning that we have found the local culture to be very different from London. In many respects, people seem to be more accepting of everything and less pushy and not so aggressive about getting what they want. This difference was illustrated to me recently when I got stuck in a local car park at Tesco for more than an hour because an accident caused traffic congestion on the M40 and other local roads. If I had been in London, no doubt drivers would have been furious and demanding Tesco management to find a way to get them unblocked from the car park without further delay. Instead, most people sat quietly in their cars with a few even smiling through the problem. There were no outbreaks of aggression at all. We were all released in due course as the congestion subsided.

I read a history of Banbury, which was very interesting. From medieval times it was very much an agricultural market town with sheep and other animals in the streets. The town was involved in various ways in the English Civil War when it appears there was some fighting around the centre. The Battle of Edgehill was fought nearby in 1642 with Oliver Cromwell, the leader of the Parliamentarians, staying at Ye Olde Reine Deer Inn in the town before this battle. Many historians have concluded that the outcome of the battle was a draw between the Royalists and the Parliamentarians. I have also been interested in the facts and myths behind the nursery rhyme regarding the 'fine lady' and Banbury Cross. It appears that historically there were three crosses – the market cross, a bread cross and a white cross, the last of these three being located near to where we live. The Puritans in the seventeenth century destroyed them all as unbefitting for believers, although the Victorians built a new monument, which stands at the top of the High Street today. There is no satisfactory evidence of the identity of the 'fine lady' from the nursery rhyme, although there has been speculation that she was a member of a local noble family or, alternatively, Lady Godiva.

In the nineteenth and twentieth centuries, various industries were located in the town, including some engineering firms. Parts of the Spitfire aeroplane were built here during the Second World War and various light industry has continued in the town until the present. Regarding the future, there are plans to expand the population considerably, taking advantage of the transport links, including the M40 motorway (opened in 1991) and the railway, as some trains can get to London in under one hour. On every side of Banbury, there are lots of new housing developments with plenty of properties available at rather inflated prices. The planners, however, seem to have approved these new developments without ensuring that they are accompanied by all the necessary additional community facilities. I would add that the local politics until recently were definitely dominated by the Conservatives. The local Conservative member of parliament when we moved to Banbury had a large majority at recent general elections and Cherwell Council also has a Conservative majority. It was the first time that the place where I live has had such a Conservative majority since I was living in Wokingham, Berkshire, as a teenager. However, the general election of 2024 was to change the political complexion with a Labour Party member being elected as the new member of parliament.

In recent years, we have also had opportunities to explore the wider surrounds, including attending a Thai Festival in Oxford and visiting for the first time Leamington Spa, only a few miles up the M40, which is a very pleasant town with an interesting history. Additionally, we have also spent more time in various areas of the Cotswolds that we had not visited before. It is indeed a special place, which very much reflects William Blake's description of our country as a 'green and pleasant land'.

We have also been fortunate to make some new friends in the local area, including developing links with a network of Thai women, whom Parinya has been able to befriend. She meets regularly with a small group of them to socialise and eat food. Other existing friendships with Thai women and their partners have also continued, with various people visiting us in Banbury from London. Our friend Noy, who as mentioned earlier comes originally from rural Thailand but is now director of a London City bank, has been several times with her husband Denis. We have been visited as well by Neil, the Chelsea fan, who lived near our flat in London. Additionally, we remain in regular contact with John, my long-term friend, now living in Chiang Mai.

One year after we moved to Banbury, Parinya's brother Pairote and his wife were able to leave Thailand to take a fortnight's holiday here, having obtained the necessary visas. We were able to show them some of the sights, including a weekend in London, Bath, Stratford-upon-Avon, Oxford, the Cotswolds and the Lake District. The London marathon was being held on our weekend in London, so we were all able to watch it and encourage the runners while we were all staying in Greenwich in Noy's flat. They were also able to see the usual sights, such as Trafalgar Square and the House of Commons. The trips to the Cotswolds included Bibury and Bourton-on-the-Water. In the Lake District, as well as seeing Windermere, Grasmere and Ullswater, we travelled west to rugged Wastwater. Pairote considered the Wastwater trip a highlight of their holiday. Overall, they very much enjoyed the visit to England and are keen to come back. They did indeed return several years later for another holiday with their two teenage sons.

After Pirote and Pu's first visit to England, they returned the favour when we were in Thailand later in the year by taking us in Pairote's jeep to Laos. We spent a pleasant night in the Champasak Grand Hotel, Pakse, on the banks of the River Mekong, at surprisingly low cost. We then visited various waterfalls the following day and stayed on an island on the River Mekong. Laos is one of the poorest countries in Asia and relies considerably on Chinese aid. We thought the people we met were welcoming and friendly. We finished the return trip to Thailand with a visit to some ancient rock paintings in Ubon. They were impressive.

# 19.
# THE COVID-19 PANDEMIC

When Parinya visited Thailand for the first time in nearly two and a half years from the start of the epidemic, she still had to take a PCR test on arrival there to check for possible Covid. Fortunately, it was negative and she was able to carry on with visiting her family and undertaking necessary business. Overall, we were told in the UK in 2022 that we were at the end of the main pandemic and that we had to live with the virus, which is of course still circulating in the community until the present day.

For a considerable period, I was reluctant to discuss our experience of Covid in writing. Neither of the two of us had so far caught the virus and it seemed it might be tempting fate to write about it. We recognised of course that, armed with several vaccinations each, the danger of getting a severe illness requiring hospitalisation, or of even dying, had been very substantially diminished, but we were still at least a little afraid of being infected by it. This was the legacy we were then experiencing from the last two years of the pandemic with its lockdowns, family tragedies, deaths, heroic activity by NHS staff and the vaccine creators, alongside some government incompetence and the failure of the prime minister and others to abide at times by the rules they had set for everybody else.

We accepted the need for a lockdown in March 2020 and obeyed the rules and guidelines that had been set. We thought then and now that it was in everybody's interest to comply if the spread of Covid was to be controlled and the number of people getting seriously ill and dying was to be limited as much as possible. A lockdown seemed sensible to protect the NHS while early work was undertaken in the UK and elsewhere to produce an effective vaccine. Along with many people, we were out in the street every week clapping the NHS and watching the briefings by ministers, medics and scientific advisers held regularly at 10 Downing Street.

Even during those early days of the pandemic, I realised that there were serious problems with aspects of the government's response. While recognising that knowledge about Covid-19 and its transmission was limited in spring 2020, the first lockdown should have taken place weeks earlier, and this delay in my view and that of many other people cost many thousands of lives. The decision also at that time then to discharge many elderly people from hospitals to care homes without testing for Covid was disastrous and again almost certainly led to tens of thousands of deaths. This bad decision highlighted the fact that social care as usual was treated as less a priority than NHS care, despite the reassurance from the government that residential homes were being fully protected. It was a lie.

How did we emotionally cope with early lockdowns? In the circumstances, quite well I think, although our response was complicated, as Parinya was still working part time as a 'key worker' in the café kitchen of a local supermarket and thus was more at risk of catching the virus. As I was 71 years old at the time, I was also more vulnerable to the likelihood of being seriously ill if I caught it, so I felt the need to protect myself from the virus as much as possible. Being isolated from friends was also emotionally difficult, although this was more an issue for Parinya than me, as in the past I have been quite used to having periods coping on my own. At least Parinya was able to stay in contact with everybody by her use of Messenger, Facebook, and other social media. Like most people, we had to develop some new routines to function adequately. In practical terms, we started to order most food online for delivery to the house and subscribed to Netflix to increase our entertainment options. We were also fortunate in being able to make use of our lovely garden, which Parinya had developed in previous years, with its pleasant lawn and many flowers, including the daffodils, bluebells, tulips, and roses at different times of the year. We enjoyed the company of many wild birds as well, which we have described above, such as robins, blackbirds, blue tits, and sparrows, who were regularly at our bird feeders. Being able to spend time in the spring and summer sitting in the garden was certainly a blessing in such difficult times!

Additionally, I did even more reading, including getting to grips with Joseph Conrad's novels for the first time. I was impressed by him as an artist, although much less impressed by his general political understanding and values. His anti-colonial insights in *Nostromo* and *Heart of Darkness*, however, I did find very interesting. Overall, despite our isolation during the early lockdowns, I was able at least to comfort myself that the experience was at least much better than being in prison!

The later lockdowns were emotionally easier to adjust to, although still difficult given our previous experience. Between lockdowns, we did at least manage to attend a Thai friend's marriage ceremony in London in September 2020 and the subsequent reception held in a pub next to the River Thames in Greenwich. It was a calculated risk attending, but fortunately, our two days spent in London (staying in a hotel) passed without problems and it was lovely to be at Noy's wedding. We did experience Christmas 2020 on our own, but it was fine, as we had sometimes had Christmas just by ourselves before. In January 2021, I had my first Astra

Zeneca vaccine and later on during 2021, both of us were to become fully vaccinated. During the summer of 2021, when not subject to lockdown, this gave us more confidence in travelling and we did spend one week in Devon and Cornwall and another week in the Highlands of Scotland, touring by car. We always enjoy both places and we did have a good time on both these trips.

However, the continuing lockdowns in 2021 were not without their emotional toll and in June 2021, Parinya decided to leave her employment with the local supermarket. This decision was in part due to experiences during the pandemic and some issues as well that had arisen within the management and staff team. In addition, it was also partly due to some continuing nerve problems in her left leg still causing her some discomfort and pain arising from a serious episode of sciatica experienced by Parinya the previous year. She had worked for the supermarket part time in both London and Banbury for approximately 15 years.

In December 2021 on Boxing Day, we had our friends Noy and Denis stay from London for a couple of nights just before a final lockdown period. It was a delight to see their young daughter, Clara, who was only one year old at the time. Parinya also started a new job as a part-time cook in December 2021, working in the centre of Banbury for a hotel chain. However, she was only to stay there a few months, as she then resigned, mainly because of inadequate staffing and support in April 2022 just after all the Covid restrictions were fully removed.

Despite the high incidence of Covid continuing in the community, we were pleased to be able to return, albeit with some caution, to a more 'normal' life in spring 2022. At that time, neither of us had contacted Covid or been faced with a family or personal crisis or tragedy due to the epidemic of the virus during the previous two years, but it had certainly still been a very difficult period.

It was at the end of April 2022, Parinya visited Thailand for the first time since late 2019. She required a Thai Pass with proof of vaccinations and had to test for Covid on arrival and again after five days. Fortunately, she was negative and was able to continue with visits and activities, although one brother had contacted Covid when she arrived in her village and had been told to isolate. Overall, the trip went well, although there were some delays and queues in Bangkok at the airport when she was returning.

In June, we had a few days again in Cornwall and then in July had a package holiday for a week to Chamonix and Mont Blanc in France. It was great seeing the Alps and we climbed to more than 10,000 feet in cable cars. But it was in coming back to the UK, that our luck in terms of Covid avoidance ran out. I developed a cough and a cold on the way home and on the following morning took a lateral flow test, which was positive. I felt unwell for a few days and as well as a cough and a cold had unusually for me a bad headache. Parinya tested positive a few days later after developing a sore throat and more generally feeling unwell. Fortunately, we both recovered after a few days. It was not surprising that we caught it, as when in Chamonix, very few people were wearing masks and some of the lifts in the mountains had up to fifty people squeezed together!

# 20.
# LIFE AFTER COVID-19

So, life continued. In autumn 2022 we took a trip to Blackpool to see the Illuminations. I recall being told by my parents that I had visited Blackpool as a child when we still lived in Lancashire, but I had rarely been there since and Parinya had taken an immediate dislike to the town on her only visit there. Unfortunately, the Queen had died the day before our planned visit and the Illuminations were cancelled on that Friday night. We did see them unlit but of course it was not quite the same! We had other plans in the Peak District for the day after when the lights were back on again. Probably I will never see them now.

We also managed a few days staying back in London, courtesy of our friends Noy and Denis, who were away at the time. It was strange in some ways being back in London, but we did manage to see some old friends and take the opportunity to behave like tourists, going to the top of The Shard and Sky Garden (another skyscraper in the city) and visiting the theatre. We also spent time in Greenwich Park, which was one of our favourite places when we lived in London. The main drawback was travelling on crowded trains and a very busy Underground to get about while staying there.

We had bad news as well about our friend John, who was still living in Chiang Mai. He informed us that he had just split from his wife Knight, to whom he had been married for about three years, and that they would be getting a divorce. He said it was amicable and they had reached a settlement. Among other things, he would be keeping the dog! At least he has his band to keep him busy. He continues to sing a good version of 'The House of the Rising Sun'. We were of course concerned and hoped that we would see him soon.

In the autumn of 2022, Parinya started to apply for part-time jobs again. She became interested in a catering post at our local hospice for terminally ill patients in a village near Banbury. We learnt that the hospice had been set up as a charity in the 1990s. It is now operated in a close partnership with the NHS, which provided more financial assistance for a period following difficulties that arose during the Covid-19 pandemic. Following a very extensive and bureaucratic NHS recruitment process and two interviews, Parinya was appointed as a cook and commenced work in early December 2022. The managers and staff teams are very friendly and so far she is enjoying this new work experience. All the meals must be prepared to a high-quality standard to meet the individual needs of the terminally ill patients. Great care must also be taken regarding allergies and other specific requirements. As I write this, she is still working at the hospice after more than two years, although her employment is now with the hospice rather than with the NHS.

So everyday life carries on. Who knows what our lives will bring in the coming months and years…

# 21.
# REFLECTIONS ON LOVE, FRIENDSHIP, SOCIETY, HEROES/ANTI-HEROES

There have certainly been several major crises in my personal life, but overall, I feel quite lucky and contented with how it has all turned out. For that outcome, I must overwhelmingly thank my lovely wife, Parinya, whom I met more than 23 years ago. In some ways, maybe I rescued her, but she also rescued me by giving me her love and bringing much-needed stability to my life. Previously, I had always thought that I was living my life on the edge and that one event might send me crashing to goodness knows where. In my case, it is true that I saved the best for last.

I would also like to thank everyone who helped me enjoy my life and become at least a little less serious as I got older. I certainly had more fun later, after my rather serious childhood, and came to experience a lot more humour, especially with my long-term friend John and other people we knew. Our various adventures together, albeit often fuelled by alcohol, have certainly been special and hopefully we can continue them for a few more years yet. We have had a really good time and a laugh whether it was abroad in Greece or Spain or more recently in Thailand, or while in Nottingham or elsewhere in the UK. As part of these adventures, we definitely had a few narrow escapes but fortunately have managed to survive them all. I would certainly like to raise a glass to the importance of friendship.

There were four major crises in my life: the ending of my affair with Lorna, Mandy's death from the overdose, the drink-driving incident, and much later, the bowel cancer. I lived through all of them, albeit not without considerable difficulty. But, as they say, anything you survive makes you stronger. I think it has been true in my case.

Of course, I have also relied a lot on friendship. I believe that in my early years, some friendships helped to make up for the feelings I had that everything in my life was temporary, given the twelve homes I had experienced before my teenage years ended. These friendships also helped me to make some sense of what happened at home with my parents and at my various schools. It was not an unhappy childhood but the lack of emotional closeness to my father had significant effects, even though I believe he did love me. I was never in any doubt about my mother's love but, as I have mentioned above, her nervousness affected me in various ways as well. I was too serious, introverted and lacking confidence in social situations, and I needed to develop more of a sense of humour. On the other hand, as a teenager, I certainly came to experience an increasing belief in my intellectual abilities. My friendships during the period I was at university developed my social skills, and my later relationship with John and others helped me to some extent become less serious and led to a lot of fun times. In many respects, my personality was the opposite of John's, as he took very few matters seriously. In this way, we complemented each other.

With regard to wider issues about our place in the world and what it all means, I came to develop at the London School of Economics in my late teens and early 20s a political perspective that I have never really lost and which I could perhaps describe as libertarian, socialist and internationalist, although I am increasingly reluctant in truth to identify with any labels. I recognise though that claiming such a perspective would no doubt be described by some people as contradictory in at least some respects, given possible tensions between ensuring maximum individual freedom and developing an effective social state, healthier communities and improved environments, and bringing about ever-closer international cooperation and partnerships. In reality, however, I do not accept there is such a contradiction, as human potential and freedom will not be fully realised without social interventions to reduce inequalities, the creation of improved and greener environments that are more in harmony with nature, and the further development of international law and regional and international institutions. In my view, unmodified capitalism will never enable these various goals to be fully achieved in the longer term, as its very basis is the pursuit of profit and capital accumulation, which for many people both limits the opportunities for individual development and denies social justice and greater equality. Therefore, capitalism must be substantially modified by both the social state and international partnerships if we are to achieve a better world. Major new controls and regulation and radical fiscal policies are still very much required to modify capitalism in a way that can serve most of the people, rather than the situation at present when it is only a small minority that receive most of the benefits from their ownership of capital. The market economy, with greater regulation, should continue to have an important role to play, but it must operate alongside a strong public sector and a more powerful social enterprise and charity sector.

I do believe that even in the short to medium term it is still possible to mitigate the worst negative effects of capitalism by improved education with more equal opportunities, by returning to more radical progressive taxation policies, and by the pursuing in a radical way the further development of a social state. In fact, fiscal policies and taxation in Western Europe and the United States were generally more progressive after the Second World War, particularly between 1945 and 1980, but since then such approaches have been reversed by more unbridled competition and market-orientated policies, which have been allowed to dominate government policies during the last 40 years. We are now living in more unequal societies than before 1980, both as demonstrated in terms of the share of national income for the rich, the middle classes, and the poor, and in the distribution of national wealth. Professor Thomas Piketty's recent books mentioned below on the role of capital provide a comprehensive analysis of what has been happening worldwide and sketch some proposals about how the current situation might be improved if there is the political will and sufficient support to do so.

To reiterate, my left-wing political beliefs were forged during my time at London School of Economics. Soon afterwards, I rejected mainstream labourism and aspects of social democracy as being largely ineffective and communism in its institutional guises as being too authoritarian, dogmatic and undemocratic. I had already before then rejected religious belief intellectually while still at school, although I have since always accepted pragmatically Bertolt Brecht's perspective that if religion would make you a better person, then you probably should start believing! I came to be sympathetic to Marx's view of religion as the 'opium of the masses', but I have also remained firmly of the view that freedom of worship must always be fully protected. With respect to my own personal view regarding religion, I have always been an agnostic rather than an atheist, even though I consider it highly unlikely that any supreme spirit or being exists. The intellectual arrogance of atheism seemed to me to contradict Socrates's aphorism, which I agree with, 'that the wise man is the man who knows he knows nothing'. Some intellectual humility seems appropriate.

Anyway, as detailed above, I adopted a Trotskyist perspective for a while, but after a short period, I felt unable to practise what was required by the theory. I also increasingly realised that I disagreed with aspects of the theory, as Trotskyism still entailed rule by a party elite without genuine democratic accountability or safeguards. Additionally, I was unable to see the world in such black and white terms as required by the theory. There were too many shades of grey in my experience. I suppose, also, I came to be distrustful about various aspects of human nature. I perhaps somewhat reluctantly concluded that I would always in the future be a democrat, accepting the old saying that democracy is far from perfect but it is better than all the other alternatives.

However, I never really thought that joining the Labour Party would be an appropriate step for me given my extremely critical views of Labourism in power, although for a while I did still vote for them. I did believe, and still do, that the only period that the Labour Party has pursued radical policies in office was after the Second World War with the development of the National Health Service and the welfare state. 'War is the locomotive of history', as Trotsky once said. Otherwise, the Labour Party's record in office in the twentieth century was tainted with compromise and sometimes betrayal as Ralph Miliband's brilliant book *Parliamentary Socialism* details. Although later Labour governments did bring about important social reforms (for example, on abortion and homosexuality), introducing the minimum wage, and the achievement with other partners of peace in Ireland, the overall record is very disappointing. They have attempted basically to manage capitalism better than the Conservatives, especially under New Labour, rather than introduce a radical policy agenda that really tackles inequality and strives to obtain social justice. The truth is that they have in fact in many ways failed in the task they set themselves. Even worse, Tony Blair took us into a criminal conspiracy with George Bush, the US president, which led to an illegal and unjustified war in Iraq. I stopped voting for the Labour Party when Tony Blair became prime minister. I should add that I have never felt that I could join any other political party, although I do have substantial sympathy with some of the more radical policies of the liberal democrats, especially in the areas regarding the protection of individual freedoms and the importance of limiting state power. I am also attracted by some of the policies of the Green Party.

Our democracy though definitely needs radical reform if it is to genuinely offer new opportunities with more progressive policies to be introduced and fully implemented. As well as the need for proportional representation, political party finance requires major changes so that funding is not dependent mainly on the contributions of the rich major companies and the trade unions. Action is also required to stop the national press and some other media being owned by a small number of billionaires and millionaires, who use such ownership to disseminate their own views when they often do not even live in this country. Additionally, major fiscal reform involving much more progressive income and inheritance taxes and a new wealth tax will be essential if a fairer, less unequal society is to be achieved. These initiatives should also be complemented by a major reform of the education system which limits the role of private education and provides radical incentives for the integration of public and private schools. There can be no substantial moves to a much more equal society without substantial new restrictions on private education. Finally, further health service and social care reform is desperately required so that more integrated quality provision, adequately funded, is delivered for everybody

Racism and other forms of discrimination must also still be tackled effectively. When I opposed the presence of the National Front in the East End of London in the 1970s, I would certainly have expected by now that more radical progress would have been made than has occurred in nearly half a century. Working in Greenwich for many years, the lessons that should have been learnt from Stephen Lawrence's tragic death by white racists also comes to mind. There can be no better society for all of us if racism, sexism and other forms of discrimination are not tackled effectively. As someone who worked for many years with people with learning disabilities, I also want to emphasise the importance of taking more convincing action against the continuing discrimination experienced by disabled people. In my view, to make much greater progress in all these areas, the significance of continuing class discrimination has to be understood as well and then acted upon. The huge discrepancies of different social groups in the level of ownership of capital must be tackled if an effective action plan for reducing inequality is to be implemented. There can, I believe, be no comprehensive and fully effective solution to overcoming all these types of discrimination without implementing a radical economic and social programme to substantially modify capitalism.

Support for parliamentary democracy does not of course preclude the importance of other political action apart from parliaments and any other elected bodies. Demonstrations and other street and local politics continue to be very important if politics is to thrive and be effective. Many of us may not have been involved in this way during much of our lives but we will have to be more engaged if we are to achieve the outcomes in society that we seek.

However, I must say as well that events in the last decade such as the result of the UK referendum on membership of the European Union and Donald Trump's first and now second period as President of the United States have disturbed me and led me to reflect on the dangers of various kinds of populist politics. I recall that it was the ancient Greeks and Romans who understood the perils arising from demagoguery. I hope that people in the future, if not seemingly in the present, will have the sense to resist the lies of populist politicians seeking power and using the politics of fear, excessive nationalism and xenophobia to achieve their ends. I am not confident that this will happen. Recent events have highlighted for me yet again the dangerous irrationality at times of human behaviour. When the genie is let out of the bottle, we must worry about the consequences. As a young man, I believed perhaps naively that politics could be increasingly rational and that in some ways Fascism had been an aberration. I remember arguing with my history teacher, (as I mentioned above), who had said that 'all men live by their illusions'. I claimed then that to progress we all had to live by the truth. This belief in the triumph of reason of course arising from the Enlightenment was supported by both liberal and socialist ideologies. It seemed an acceptable assumption at the time, but I now believe there can be no such complacency about continuing progress and that the forces of irrationality must be continually fought if they are to be defeated. For me, excessive nationalism remains an extremely dangerous force in our world. If anything, at the beginning of the twenty-first century, this force has become more powerful as examples of the activities of countries such as China, India, Russia, Turkey and the United States have been demonstrating only too well. In my view, such nationalism also continues to be a dangerous force in our own country, which is still leading to irrational decision-making based on a continuing illusion that we are much more powerful as a nation than we are. I should add that this illusion for a significant number of people continues to be accompanied by overt or more covert racist beliefs. We have not yet fully rid ourselves of our Empire mentality.

The most obvious example of these dangers in our own country, which in my view illustrates only too well this irrationality, is demonstrated in the result of the EU referendum in 2016 and its aftermath. While I still consider the EU to be essentially a capitalist club, the decision to leave it and deprive ourselves of an accessible economic market without tariffs involving several hundred million people will, I believe, inevitably result in us being worse off overall. Even in terms of politics and the argument to take 'back control', I have come across no convincing evidence that leaving the EU will achieve such a goal. On the contrary, it is almost certain that as a nation we will finish up having less influence and power in the world. We will only be stronger if we operate closely together and in partnership with our near neighbours. Any other conclusion is nostalgia for our past and the Empire and wishful thinking. Preserving the peace in Europe also requires this unity, even if it is becoming an increasing struggle to maintain it and protect human rights and democracy. I despair of the people who seem to lack any sense of history and do not appear to understand the fragility of peace in Europe following the many hundreds and thousands of years of war and destruction on our continent. As I review these thoughts and this text, we have now been apart from the European Union for more than five years and I worry a lot about what the future will bring for all of us.

Following the decision on Brexit, and bearing in mind Donald Trump's elections as president, I also have substantial concerns about the extremist right populist forces that may be unleashed in various parts of Europe and elsewhere in the coming years. For example, we already have the worrying examples of the neo-fascist party led by Marine Le Pen, which has been doing well in the French presidential elections and the authoritarian undemocratic nationalist regimes in Poland and Hungary. There is also increasing support for extreme right parties in Germany and Italy. They are already in government in Italy. I just hope that we learn some of the lessons from history in time. We should be in no doubt that new forms of authoritarian rule, excessive nationalism, and Fascist-type leadership with accompanying racism are becoming more powerful forces across the world. We must unite to challenge and defeat them.

So... what is my identity? I do not identify with any particular location, but I certainly regard myself as

English in the sense of William Blake's 'green and pleasant land.' I am a UK citizen but not 'British' as the latter description will be for ever in my mind be associated with the British Empire and colonialism. I also consider myself a European, which is perhaps one of the reasons why I remain so upset about leaving the European Union, as the departure has involved losing part of my overall identity. I am also pleased to call myself a citizen of the world – despite some people's derogatory comments that such a statement means you are a citizen of nowhere. On the contrary, it means something to me, particularly in terms of common humanity and experiencing a shared environment and planet. We all have a responsibility to protect the world's animals and plants, other aspects of the environment and to prevent as much as we can any substantial climate change. The need for radical action in these areas is pressing, but international political action has so far been entirely inadequate. To date, humanity has failed to tackle these huge problems in any way effectively and as I write, there is little evidence that we will do better in the future.

Moving on, who have been my heroes or maybe sometimes anti-heroes? In this regard, I am partly thinking about those individuals who have inspired me with their knowledge and insight and those who combined such understanding with action to inspire me, and others, and sometimes provide leadership towards making the world a better place. I am also thinking about people who have best understood human frailty but have recognised that it sometimes can be combined with heroic behaviour and true greatness. These characters may still be regarded as inadequate and as failures by some but for me they are often the real heroes. My list consists of literary figures, academics, and a few men and women of action. Some of them have had a greater influence on me at different stages of my life and others I feel have been very much alongside me throughout my time here. Everyone will have their own personal list of heroes of course.

Firstly, I would choose Fyodor Dostoevsky for his excellence in writing novels that provide both brilliant psychological insight into how the human mind and emotions operate and his great understanding of how social circumstances influence how we all behave. His insights are as valuable now as when the novels were written in the nineteenth century. I recall reading *Crime and Punishment* when I was still an undergraduate at university and being immensely impressed with his insights into human nature. No wonder Einstein stated that he learnt more from Dostoevsky than anyone else. And Nietzsche said that he discovered more insights from Dostoevsky than all psychologists combined. The genius of Dostoevsky has also been brought home to me recently by my reading of Leo Tolstoy's two great works *War and Peace* and *Anna Karenina*. While in no way doubting the greatness of Tolstoy's novels, with his great understanding of the Russian nobility and peasantry and his many insights into love and the wider human condition, he does not for me manage to achieve the psychological intuitive understanding of human beings of different groups and classes demonstrated by Dostoevsky. I think Dostoevsky is the greatest of all novelists.

Secondly, near the top my list would be Vasily Grossman, another Russian novelist, who in my view is one of the finest writers in the last one hundred years. His epic novel, *Life and Fate,* on the battle of Stalingrad and so much more regarding the human condition in the twentieth century is the recent equivalent of Tolstoy's *War and Peace*. He has an empathetic understanding of human relationships and emotions. A prequel to this novel entitled *Stalingrad* has in recent times been re-edited and published in English. As a Jewish journalist operating under Stalin's dictatorship, his *War Diaries* are also fascinating, as are some of his earlier writings. The description in his article about entering the Treblinka death camp at the end of the Second World War is both harrowing and full of human compassion. Above all, it is this humanity and his moral compass that light up his writings.

Thirdly, I would have to include the historian Eric Hobsbawm, whom I mentioned earlier, whose specialist area of study for most of his life was the nineteenth century. From reading *The Age of Revolution,* with its profound analysis of both the Industrial Revolution and the French Revolution, while still at school, I have always been full of admiration for all his writings. I believe that he was undoubtedly the greatest historian of the twentieth century because of his brilliant political, economic, social and cultural analysis and his ability to convincingly bring all these areas together in a coherent way. He was as erudite about historical aspects of the arts and science as he was regarding the more usual analysis of political, social and economic developments. He wrote not just about European history but also about world history – hence his continuing popularity in countries such as India and Brazil. While he was a Marxist throughout his life, he did not let his theoretical perspective restrict in any way his analysis. Indeed, it led to much greater understanding and many new insights. For example, his book *Bandits* offered a major new analysis of the social movements connected with the activities of some of the most famous outlaws. He also led a fascinating early life with his Jewish family, who were living in Berlin during the rise of Nazism but then moved to England when he was a teenager. More than anyone else he has helped me understand our recent history.

Fourth on my list would be the novelist Graham Greene, for creating *Greeneland*, which again provides great insights into human nature. While some critics have dismissed the world he describes in his novels with its anti-heroes as too dark, pessimistic and full of shades of grey, I believe that many of his characters offer a deep understanding of various aspects of human life, relationships and emotions. His novels *The Power and the Glory, The Honorary Consul* and *The Heart of the Matter* are especially important in this regard, although there is much to appreciate and admire in many of his other writing. His anti-heroes combine all kinds of human weakness with sometimes unexpected strength and compassion when it really matters. He led a full and interesting life, from his early experience playing Russian roulette, his marriage and conversion to Catholicism, to his various travel adventures, his love affair with Kathryn, his activities as a British spy, his friendships with revolutionaries and dictators, and his later life with a partner living on the Isle of Capri, and the end of his life spent in Switzerland. His novel *The End of the Affair* was particularly important to me, as Lorna and I both liked it and discussed it. I regarded it as *our* novel. I remember crying at a railway station in the West Country when I bought a newspaper and learnt of Graham Greene's death in 1991.

Fifth on my list is Rosa Luxembourg, the socialist and revolutionary, who along with Karl Liebknecht helped lead the German socialist opposition to the First World War, and who understood only too well that the choice for the human race at that time was between 'socialism or barbarism'. She was not only a leading theoretician of socialism in the early part of the twentieth century but provided important leadership when most social democrats in Germany embraced unquestioning nationalism and followed the Kaiser to war. As a leader of the Spartacists, she died fighting for a better world, murdered by the Freikorps militia consisting of nationalists and ex-army gangs after the Great War ended. Undoubtedly, her murderers and many people with similar views would later be joining the Nazi Party and contributing to the rise of Fascism and Hitler.

The sixth person on my list would be Francisco Sabaté Llopart, the Spanish anarchist, who refused to accept the tragic defeat of the Republican forces in the Spanish Civil War. He continued for many years a one-man armed struggle against Franco's regime with regular raids into Spain in the period from 1939–1957 until his luck ran out on a trip to Barcelona and he was shot and killed. He was the quintessential man of action in the fight against right wing nationalism and Fascism who continued the struggle in Spain when almost everyone else had ceased. His propaganda of the deed continues to inspire, although his actions at the time were ultimately doomed to failure. I recall reading Eric Hobsbawm's account of his life in *Bandits* and admiring him ever since then. I discuss more about the importance of the Spanish Civil War to my thinking and outlook below.

My seventh choice would have to be David Attenborough, naturalist, broadcaster and writer, for his lifelong inspiring study of animals and plants, and the knowledge and experience he has provided us with through his many books and TV broadcasts. He has communicated his love of nature as well as his serious concerns about what human beings have been doing to the natural world in a special way. I was brought up on some of his Zoo Quest books, including *Zoo Quest in Paraguay*, and I feel he has always been one of my important companions. In his ninth decade, he continues to inspire us with his campaigns to counter climate change and environmental destruction.

Eighth, I must include Albert Einstein for both his scientific genius that has helped us understand much better the marvels of our universe and his overall contribution as a human being and internationalist. He provides a wonderful example of what can be achieved with a systematic search for knowledge, even without necessarily having a traditional university education, as his greatest discoveries were made of course away from a university setting. His brilliant insights into mass, energy and time in our universe, changed physics and our understanding of the world forever. He was also a great humanitarian and supporter of global peace initiatives, including world government.

Ninth, I must mention Nelson Mandela for his great achievement in securing a free and democratic South Africa and bringing apartheid to an end. Like many people, I consider that his great personal sacrifices to achieve this end, including his lengthy imprisonment, and his other outstanding personal qualities, particularly his leadership skills, patience, humility, and abilities to forgive and enable reconciliation, mark him out as the outstanding political leader of my lifetime. To overcome the apartheid regime without a full-scale civil war was the political achievement of the twentieth century.

Finally, in terms of recent intellectual brilliance that has inspired me I would also like to mention Thomas Picketty's important book, *Capital in the Twenty-First Century*, which was published in English in 2014. This French professor provides a brilliant understanding about how capital has accumulated historically and how in this century with a return to low economic growth rates the process of capital accumulation and the returns on that capital are substantially increasing inequality in our societies. The proportion of income arising from capital in overall national income is greater than before and the total amount of capital assets as a ratio in comparison with national income is also getting much higher. The world wars and their aftermath had substantially reduced this accumulation when considered as a ratio with national income, but it now appears that this move towards greater equality was a temporary phenomenon and we are at present getting back to the level of inequality that was present before the First World War. He describes in detail how this is happening and how he expects inequality in the future to get even worse unless remedies are identified and action is taken. By way of illustration, in the UK in 2010, the top 10 per cent of the population owned 70 per cent of the wealth and the trend is for the percentage they own to be increasing. All of us who believe that a fairer, less unequal society is essential will find his excellent analysis very worrying and disturbing. His most recent publication, *Capital and Ideology*, provides a worldwide perspective on these developments and explores the political-ideological dimensions and possible remedies in much more detail.

Regarding one other final personal thought about our recent history in the last 100 years, I would now like to turn briefly back to the Spanish Civil War and the subsequent World War involving the struggle against Fascism, because it has been so important to me when trying to give meaning to my life and times. Although I was born more than 9 years after the end of the Spanish Civil War and more than 3 years following the end of the Second World War, I believe that my beliefs and values have been shaped substantially by my understanding of these events. As I studied our recent history at university, I came to deplore the British Government's policy of non-intervention in Spain and the appeasement of the Fascist dictators in Germany, Italy and elsewhere. The betrayal of the Republican government in Spain by the British state following the military uprising which Hitler and Mussolini backed was in my view tragic, especially when compared with the action of those many volunteers, including those from the UK, who went there to join the International Brigades and the other militias and to fight and often die for the Republican cause. Despite the disgraceful actions of the Stalinists, who appear to have been as interested in destroying their socialist and anarchist allies as in fighting Franco, if ever there was a conflict where right and wrong were so clearly delineated it was in Spain at that time.

If Fascism had been defeated there, who knows what a difference it may have made to the overall struggle against Hitler and his allies. Again, if Hitler had subsequently been confronted rather than appeased in Czechoslovakia and elsewhere, twentieth-century history may have been substantially different, and less sacrifice may have been required ultimately in the struggle to overcome Fascism. I would always describe myself as an anti-fascist as well as an anti-capitalist. We should always be alert to the danger of new forms of Fascism arising again. But I am fearful that some current populist movements are taking us in that direction.

What about death? It does not worry me, although I am of course concerned that Parinya can experience a good life after I have gone. Dying of course is a different matter and I hope like everyone else that when it happens it will be reasonably peaceful, and not too dramatic or painful. To die while sleeping in one's own bed having bid goodbye to those you care about would of course be ideal. However, if this is not possible, I hope I will be able to accept without too much rancour what fate chooses for me.

Finally, I have concluded like many others that as human being, it is up to us to give life its meaning, but that we can also take some comfort from our place in nature, our planet and the wider universe, provided that in our thoughts and actions we demonstrate that we care about our world and do not abuse our position. Respecting all our fellow creatures and other aspects of our environment would be a start. I think the jury must be out about whether this hope in time can be realised or not for the human race. Overall, I have appreciated my life and have enjoyed much of it. I would like to thank everyone who has contributed positively to it. I do hope that on balance, I have also made a positive contribution to the lives of others, while recognising at times that more 'loving kindness' to quote Thomas Hardy would have been desirable. Most of all, I must thank Parinya for her love that has meant so much to me in the last 23 and more years. As I complete these reflections, I do hope that we can continue to share this love for at least a few more years yet.

~~ THE END ~~

www.ingramcontent.com/pod-product-compliance
Lightning Source LLC
LaVergne TN
LVHW011325080426
835513LV00006B/198